THE NATIONAL DEVELOPMENT PROGRAMME IN COMPUTER ASSISTED LEARNING FINAL REPORT OF THE DIRECTOR

THE NATIONAL DEVELOPMENT PROGRAMME IN COMPUTER ASSISTED LEARNING

FINAL REPORT OF THE DIRECTOR

Richard Hooper

CET The National Development Programme
in Computer Assisted Learning

Published by the Council for Educational Technology
3 Devonshire Street, London W1N 2BA

Acknowledgements: the National Development Programme gratefully acknowledges permission to print the illustrations granted by University College London (p 24); the Ministry of Defence (A Ed 2) (p 85); Napier College of Commerce and Technology (p 119); the Advisory Unit for Computer Based Education, Herts (p 143); the University of Surrey (p 145); and the Royal Naval College, Greenwich (p 158).

First published 1977
ISBN 0 902204-75-0

Printed in Great Britain by Direct Design (Bournemouth) Limited, Sturminster Newton, Dorset.

Foreword

This Report summarises the work and conclusions of a five-year National Development Programme through which the United Kingdom has established itself as one of the world leaders in computer assisted learning. At a time when educational budgets are subject to constraint it is particularly useful to have clear indications of the role of the computer in relation to teaching and learning, where and how it should and should not be applied. The Report deserves careful study by administrators and teachers alike, and will be of interest not only to the education service but also to those engaged in training in industry and the armed services.

The work of the National Development Programme has involved many groups and individuals—the Committee which steered it, the Programme Director and his staff, the educational and financial evaluators and the local project staff. We are all indebted to them for carrying out successfully a demanding and important task.

Shirley Williams
Secretary of State for Education and Science

Contents

Introduction

This is, above all, a happy story. The National Development Programme in Computer Assisted Learning (NDPCAL) has lived through a period of economic gloom, amidst increasing uncertainty about, and public disaffection with, education. Yet, I am able to report much work completed within a tight time schedule, and evidence of successful fulfilment of the Programme's major objective — the 'institutionalisation' of computer assisted learning. The existence of the Programme has, I believe, reduced wasteful duplication of activity by achieving significant transfer of both experience and teaching materials.

In recommending to the Government that the Programme should close itself down as planned, I feel that computer assisted learning (CAL) and computer managed learning (CML) are now resilient enough to face what may be an uncomfortable couple of years.

The creation of NDPCAL

It was almost exactly ten years ago that the newly formed National Council for Educational Technology (NCET) began to develop ideas for an advanced project concerning computers in education. In 1969, following extensive study, NCET recommended that the British Government should spend £2 millions over five years on a coordinated, national programme in computer-based learning. In the spring of 1972, Mrs Thatcher, Secretary of State for Education and Science, approved the Programme. It began when I took up the post of Director on 1 January 1973. The Programme was steered by an executive Programme Committee, chaired by John Hudson, Deputy Secretary in the Department of Education and Science. The Committee contained representatives of seven government departments, other national agencies, for example the Council for Educational Technology (in 1973 the National Council for Educational Technology was reconstituted to form the Council for Educational Technology for the United Kingdom — CET) and the Social Science Research Council, plus a small number of coopted advisers (see Appendix A, p 169, and Figure 1).

As Programme Director, I was principal officer to the Programme Committee and all proposals for funding came to the Committee through the Directorate. The half-dozen Directorate staff were all employees of the Council for Educational Technology (CET) and CET provided certain administrative services to the Programme, notably in the area of financial accounting.

Two agencies were contracted to undertake the independent educational and financial evaluation of the National Programme. The educational evaluation was carried out by the UNCAL team (UNderstanding Computer Assisted Learning) at the Centre for Applied Research in Education at the University of East Anglia, directed by Barry MacDonald. The financial evaluation was carried out by John Fielden, assisted by Philip Pearson, both of Peat, Marwick, Mitchell & Co, Management Consultants.

The creation of NDPCAL and its first two years of operation are covered in detail in my previous report, *Two Years On*, published by the Council for Educational Technology in 1975.

Computer assisted learning

Many people equate computer assisted learning with programmed learning, and with the provision of cost-effective teaching through the reduction of labour costs (ie fewer teachers). This image of CAL, largely inherited from North America, must be put to one side if the National Programme, and this final report, is to be understood. Computer assisted learning, and its twin, computer managed learning, as defined and developed by the Programme, are characterised by a versatility of applications, some of which have nothing to do with programmed learning at all (see Chapter 5 for definitions). Even those applications which do derive from the programmed learning tradition, for example the computer acting in a tutorial role (often called CAI, computer assisted instruction), are not very reminiscent of programmed texts. Many CAL applications involve the computer performing complex tasks, for example simulation, that cannot be done by other media (including the live teacher), and concern the qualitative, rather than quantitative, improvement of teaching.

The shape of this final report

The report is divided into four parts. Part One sets out what the Programme has achieved in relation to its main aims. Part Two contains reports from the independent evaluators on the educational potential, and costs, of CAL and CML. Part Three describes how the Programme went about its task. Part Four is concerned with the future, both short and medium-term. It contains the final conclusions of a future study carried out by the Programme on computers in education and training in the 1980s. Recommendations for central government policy in the years immediately following the Programme's closure and in the 1980s are outlined. Finally, after an epilogue, there are three appendices to the Report: membership of the Programme Committee; brief summaries of all projects and studies funded by the Programme; a select bibliography of publications produced within the Programme.

Richard Hooper
Director, NDPCAL
Summer 1977

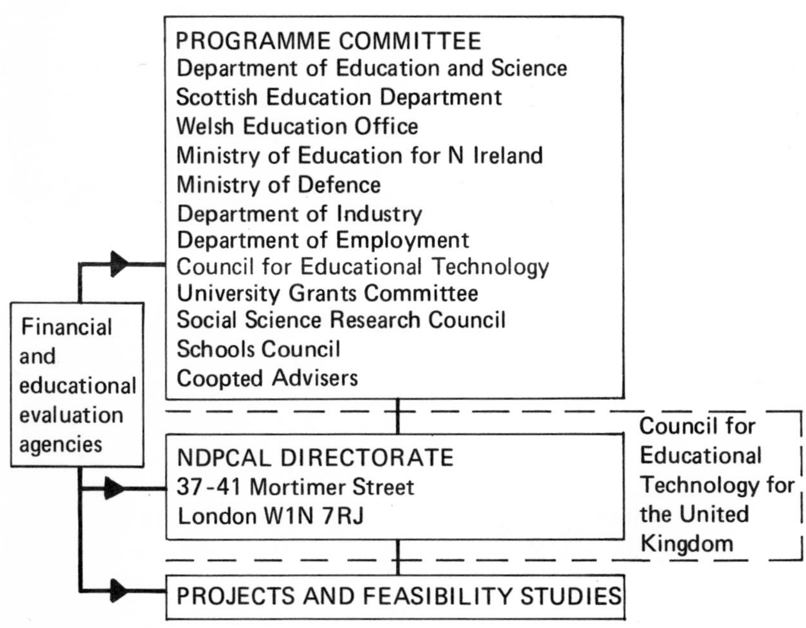

Figure 1. NDPCAL executive structure

PART ONE

THE PROGRAMME'S ACHIEVEMENTS

Chapter 1 and 2 set out the progress that has been made towards fulfilment of the Programme's twin aims of 'institutionalisation' and 'transferability'. Working CAL and CML systems, institutionalised after the end of external funding, and transferred to new institutions, are the major product of the National Programme.

1. Progress towards institutionalisation

In the first month of the first year of the Programme, the main aim for the Programme was formulated:

— to develop and secure the assimilation of computer assisted and computer managed learning on a regular institutional basis at reasonable cost.

This aim became, in NDPCAL shorthand, 'the institutionalisation of CAL and CML'. (The term 'institutionalisation' did not have unqualified support amongst Programme Committee members, because of its association with hospitals and prisons! However, no other term seemed to be quite so apt.) Institutionalisation was defined pragmatically as the successful takeover of working CAL and CML systems on to local budgets on a permanent basis after the period of external funding runs out. Thus, the primary product of the National Programme, on which it asks to be judged, is evidence of institutionalisation, not research generalisations derived from a series of experiments.

Why institutionalisation?

This aim of institutionalisation was chosen for two reasons. Firstly, given the difficulties of evaluation, institutionalisation is one measure of educational value. Secondly, when the Programme began, there was growing concern in the educational technology community at the lack of success with institutionalisation of educational innovation over the last two decades on both sides of the Atlantic. In June 1972 the influential US Carnegie Commission on Higher Education had written:

'One of the great disappointments of the national effort to date is that for all the funds and effort thus far expended for the advancement of instructional technology, penetration of new learning materials and media into higher education has thus far been shallow' (The Carnegie Commission on Higher Education, 1972, p 47).

Perhaps rather surprisingly given the acknowledgement of the problem, very few curriculum or educational technology projects have confronted it directly. The 1960s schools curriculum development projects, in the USA and the UK, tended to aim for the development of high quality teaching materials, based on appropriate definition of educational objectives and sound curriculum design. In higher education, many educational technology projects have research aims — to demonstrate the value of, for example, computer assisted learning, to prove via experiments its cost-effectiveness, to elaborate its theoretical bases.

Many of these projects tend to assume that the existence of high quality teaching materials, positive research and cost/effectiveness data, or elegant theoretical explication, will ensure that the particular innovation is institutionalised. The National Programme made no such assumption.

'The belief that innovations succeed on their merits, a belief that sustained the rational optimism of the first generation of curriculum developers, has never been much in evidence at the centre of the National Programme .... the citadel of established practice will seldom fall to the polite knock of a good idea. It may however yield to a long siege, a pre-emptive strike, a wooden horse or a cunning alliance' (MacDonald *et al* , 1975, p 49).

For a review of the various strategies adopted by the National Programme to accelerate institutionalisation of CAL and CML, see Chapter 6 in Part Three.

Institutionalisation achieved

The criterion of institutionalisation is applicable to 27 of the 35 main projects and feasibility studies funded by the Programme (listed in Figure 2, pp 18, 19). By the last year of the Programme these 27 projects involved directly 44 different institutions (a local education authority, LEA, is classed here and in the subsequent statistics as an 'institution'). Quite a number of institutions participated in more than one project; for example Plymouth Polytechnic engineers in the Engineering Sciences Project (ESP), and Plymouth Polytechnic chemists in the Computer Assisted Learning in Chemistry (CALCHEM) project.

Evidence available in the summer of 1977 would suggest that in 32 project institutions out of the 44, institutionalisation will be, or has been, achieved — 70%. This claim will need to be checked in 1978 and 1979. It is likely that some of the activities which look as if they are institutionalised will not endure. On the other hand, one or two of the projects where evidence of institutionalisation is not yet apparent (for example, because they have not been running long enough) will in fact achieve it. In general, for the purposes of this analysis, where there was uncertainty about institutionalisation being achieved, a project institution was *not* given the benefit of the doubt. Thus, erring on the side of caution, it is hoped that the claim of 70% success with institutionalisation is a fair one.

Two areas of project activity have by far the highest success rate of institutionalisation. In tertiary education, the work at 22 out of 27 project institutions seems set to survive the end of 1977. In military training six out of seven project institutions would seem likely to continue with CAL/CML. In the schools sector, four out of eight local authorities look, on the present evidence, certain to continue the work. In industrial training, neither of the two projects — at the London Business School and the Post Office — can as yet be certain about their future. Industrial training was consistently the weakest area of activity in the National Programme. It was not easy to find and fund relevant projects. However, American computer manufacturers see industrial training — rather than education — as the growth area of CAL.

The evidence of institutionalisation available in the summer of 1977 is primarily the project institutions' own future financial commitment, combined with an assessment of the numbers of teachers and teaching departments involved with the work. At Glasgow University, for example, the evidence is the existence of a university-wide CAL service, based around a £50,000 GEC 4080 computer purchased out of university funds. In addition the university has agreed to support the service with computing staff. Although there remain doubts as to whether the maths project (DP 1/10) will be institutionalised within the maths department, academic interest across medicine, physics, chemistry, education is likely to be strong enough to ensure continued activity. At Leeds University, in early 1977, Senate agreed to make three *tenured* appointments to the Computer Based Learning Project, so that the varied work in statistics, chemistry, and medicine both at Leeds University and in other cooperating institutions, will develop and spread. At Chelsea College, London, an educational computing section has been organised, and this makes provision for CAL not only for college but also secondary school activity. At Brighton Polytechnic, the local authority has agreed to fund the CAMOL development officer plus secretarial support from 1 January 1978. At the University of Surrey, the Computer Board has funded a university-wide CAL service. Surrey now has two computers 'dedicated' to CAL. In addition to computing staff, future provision has also been made for the necessary educational support. At Queen Mary College, the future funding of the Computer Assisted Teaching Unit by the College has been agreed.

Tertiary education

DP 1/01B	Computer Based Learning Project (CBLP)
DP 1/02A	Engineering Sciences Project (ESP)
DP 1/03A	Computational Physics Teaching Laboratory (CPTL)
DP 1/04A	Clinical Decision Making
DP 1/06A	Computer Assisted Learning in Chemistry (CALCHEM)
DP 1/07	The MATLAB Project
DP 1/08	CAMOL in Secondary and Tertiary Education (NUU CAMOL)
DP 1/09	Computers in the Undergraduate Science Curriculum (CUSC)
DP 1/10	Basic Mathematics
DP 1/11	Computer Assisted Learning - A University Service
FS 1/22/03A	Assessment of Student Performance and Progress (BP CAMOL)
FS 1/22/04	CAMOL in Further Education (Bradford CAMOL)

Schools

DP 2/02A	Hertfordshire Computer Managed Mathematics (HCMMP)
DP 2/03A	Computer Assisted Teaching of Remedial Reading
DP 2/04	Computer Assisted School Timetabling (CAST)
DP 2/05	The Local History Classroom Project (LHCP)
FS 2/01	Local Information Services Project (LISP)
FS 2/03	Computer Assisted Learning in Upper School Geography (CALUSG)
FS 2/04	Computer Assisted Learning in Secondary School History

Armed Services

DP 3/01	Computer Assisted Technological Education of Service Personnel (CATESP)
DP 3/02	Computer Assisted Learning in-Nuclear Science and Engineering
FS 3/01A	Computer Scheduling of REME Training
FS 3/01B	Computer Aided Planning and Scheduling
FS 3/02	Diffusion of CAL to Armed Services Users
FS 3/03A	Simulation and Fault Analysis for Radionics Instruction (SAFARI)
FS 3/22/01	Computer Managed Staff Training
FS 3/22/02	Quality Control in Military Training (Catterick CAMOL)

Industrial training

DP 4/01	Management Decision Making
FS 4/03	Computer Assisted Post Office Technician Training

Transferability

TP 22/01	Cambridge University Transferability Project
TP 22/02B	Computer Assisted Management of Learning (CAMOL)
TP 22/03	BASIC to FORTRAN Machine Translation
TP 22/04A	Physical Sciences Program Exchange (PSPE)
TP 22/05	Havering/Lothian Transferability Project
TP 22/06A	Geographical Association Package Exchange (GAPE)

Key

DP = Development Project　　FS = Feasibility Study
TP = Transferability Project　　A or B = Extended Period(s) of funding

Note: Project DP 1/05, which was cancelled, and the design studies are not listed here. See Appendix B for summaries of all projects, including DP 1/05 and the design studies.

Figure 2. NDPCAL projects and feasibility studies, 1973-1977

Figure 2 (cont). NDPCAL projects and feasibility studies, 1973-1977

Note: Project base in brackets

<table>
<tr><td></td><td colspan="6">CAL</td><td>CML</td></tr>
<tr><td rowspan="2">1. TERTIARY EDUCATION</td><td>CAL SERVICE</td><td>ENGINEERING</td><td>MATHS</td><td>MEDICINE</td><td>SCIENCE</td><td>STATISTICS</td><td rowspan="2">DP 1/08 (New University of Ulster)
FS 1/22/03A (Brighton Polytechnic)
FS 1/22/04 (Bradford College)</td></tr>
<tr><td>DP 1/11 (Surrey University)</td><td>DP 1/02A (Queen Mary College)</td><td>DP 1/07 (Napier College, Edinburgh)
DP 1/10 (Glasgow University)</td><td>DP 1/04A (Glasgow University)</td><td>DP 1/03A (Surrey University)
DP 1/06A (Leeds University)
DP 1/09 (University College London)</td><td>DP 1/01B (Leeds University)</td></tr>
<tr><td rowspan="2">2. SCHOOLS</td><td colspan="3">CAL</td><td colspan="2">CML</td><td colspan="2">ADMIN</td></tr>
<tr><td colspan="3">DP 2/05 (Suffolk LEA)
FS 2/03 (Birmingham University)
FS 2/04 (Clwyd LEA)</td><td colspan="2">DP 2/02A (Herts LEA)
DP 2/03A (S Glamorgan LEA)</td><td colspan="2">FS 2/01 (CET)
DP 2/04 (LAMSAC)</td></tr>
<tr><td>3. ARMED SERVICES</td><td colspan="3">DP 3/01 (RMCS Shrivenham)
DP 3/02 (RNC Greenwich)
FS 3/02 (NDPCAL,MOD)
FS 3/03A (RAF Locking)</td><td colspan="2">FS 3/22/01 (RAF Bracknell)
FS 3/22/02 (Royal Signals Catterick)</td><td colspan="2">FS 3/01A (REME, OSA)
FS 3/01B (RAF, OSA)</td></tr>
<tr><td rowspan="2">4. INDUSTRIAL TRAINING</td><td colspan="3">MANAGEMENT TRAINING</td><td colspan="4">TECHNICIAN TRAINING</td></tr>
<tr><td colspan="3">DP 4/01 (London Business School)</td><td colspan="4">FS 4/03 (Post Office)</td></tr>
<tr><td>5. TRANSFER-ABILITY</td><td colspan="3">TP 22/01 (Cambridge University)
TP 22/02B (NDPCAL)
TP 22/03 (Culham Laboratory)</td><td colspan="4">TP 22/04A (Wolverhampton Polytechnic)
TP 22/05 (Havering/Lothian LEA)
TP 22/06A (Loughborough University)</td></tr>
</table>

At school level, Hertfordshire County Council has agreed to fund a central team to continue the work in computer managed mathematics, after the end of external funding. In Suffolk, the authority is increasing its support for the work in history through the advisory service and the provision of appropriate computing arrangements at the Ipswich Civic College.

In military training, the computer applications at the three officer-level institutions (RMCS Shrivenham, RNC Greenwich, RAF Staff College) seem secure. The RAF Staff College's limited use of the computer for diagnostic assessment has in fact been successfully institutionalised for three years. At Catterick, Army funds were used to purchase an ICL 2903 Educational System in early 1977 so that the CAMOL project for technician training in the Royal Signals will continue.

One measure of institutionalisation, and indeed of transferability, is the basic facts and figures from projects during the academic/school years 1973/4 to 1976/7. Figure 3 shows the growth of students/pupils/trainees involved in CAL and CML, under the auspices of the Programme, from 600 in 1973/4 to 13,880 in 1976/7. This growth would suggest that the Programme has moved CAL and CML out of the small-scale experimental laboratory with a handful of students and into development. For those 13 projects that used CAL in interactive mode (ie, with terminals), a measure of student terminal hours is usually appropriate. A student terminal hour is one student sitting at a terminal for one hour. Where pairs of students are sitting at a terminal for an hour, two student terminal hours are recorded. Where more than 4 students are using one terminal (as for example in class and lecture demonstration) then student terminal hours are an inappropriate measure. Figure 4 shows the growth of student terminal hours in the 13 relevant projects from 3450 in 1973/4 to 34,410 in 1976/7. For example, the Leeds statistics project (DP 1/01B) recorded 4000 student terminal hours from 650 students in 1974/5 in the three cooperating institutions (one student: one terminal ratio). In 1976/7, 850 students clocked up 7000 student terminal hours.

Two other sets of figures are appropriate at this point. Figure 5 shows the growth of institutions directly involved in NDPCAL projects, from 11 in 1973/4 to 47 in 1976/7. Also plotted on the graph, in Figure 5, is the number of other institutions (125) which have taken over project materials. Figure 6 shows the growth of teaching staff (*not* including the hundred or so project staff funded wholly by NDPCAL) involved in CAL and CML. In 1973/4 55 teachers were preparing material, using and

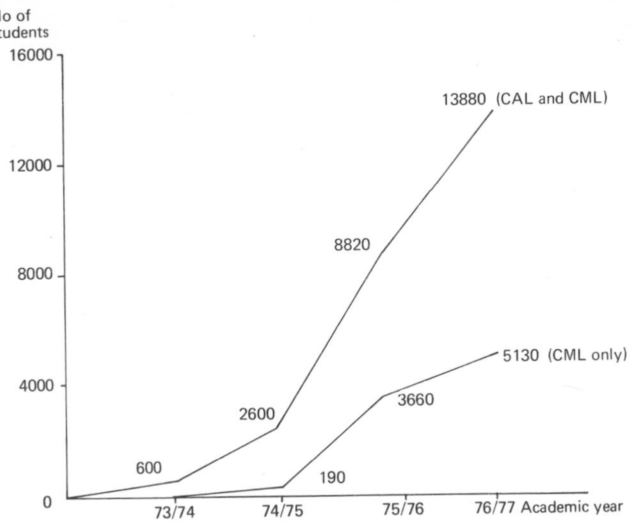

Figure 3. The number of students using CAL and CML in 17 CAL projects and 6 CML projects, 1973/4-1976/7

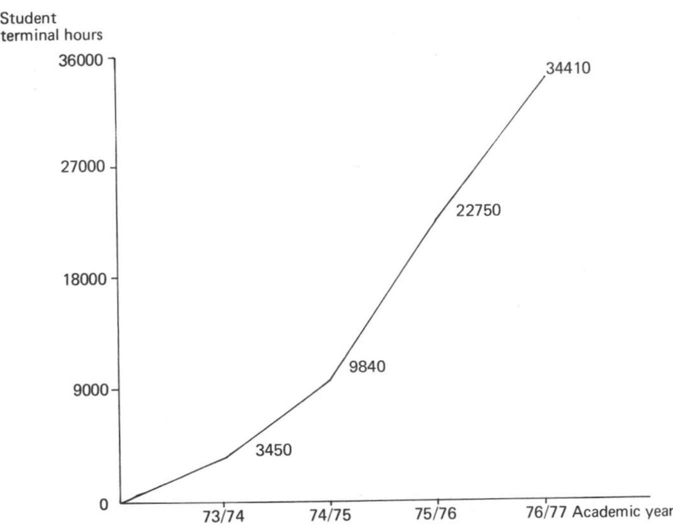

Figure 4. The number of student terminal hours in 13 relevant CAL projects, 1973/4-1976/7

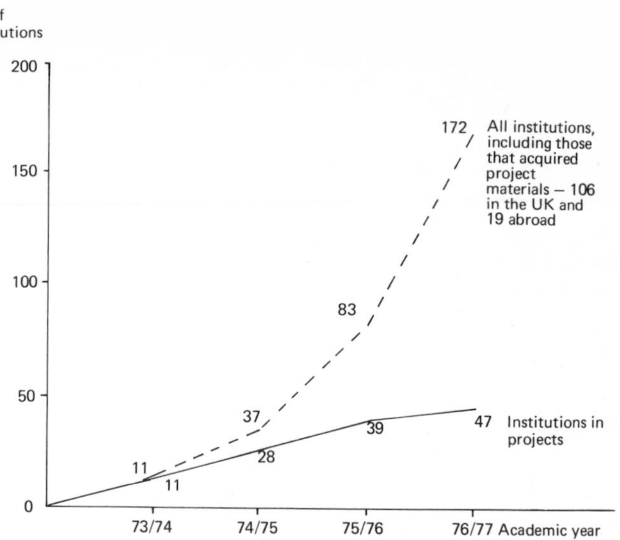

Figure 5. The number of institutions directly involved in NDPCAL projects, and other institutions acquiring project materials, 1973/4-1976/7

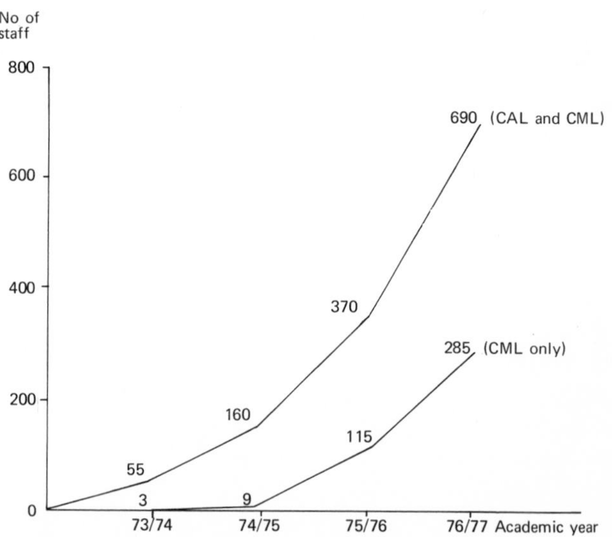

Figure 6. The number of teaching staff involved in NDPCAL projects, 1973/4-1976/7 — NDPCAL-funded staff are not included in these figures

evaluating it. By 1976/7 the number had grown to 690. This may be the best measure of institutionalisation, and of transferability, given the key role played by teachers in furthering or killing an educational or training innovation.

The statistics given in Figures 3-6 must be treated with some caution. Measures such as student terminal hours are not very accurate. Also the aggregation of figures from widely varying project environments and diverse applications of the computer is of only limited value. Nevertheless, scrutiny of such global statistics does give useful insight into the success or failure of projects and demonstrates the quickening of pace evident in the later stages of development.

One aspect of institutionalisation is the 'fate' of NDPCAL-funded project staff. On present evidence, it looks as if 20-30 of the 100 will continue to be directly involved in CAL and CML. For example, the NDPCAL-funded CAMOL coordinator (TP 22/02B) has accepted a post in CAL at Imperial College. The Open University has appointed a chemist/programmer from the CALCHEM project (DP 1/06A) to continue work on CAL begun at Leeds University.

Finally, a very large quantity of teaching materials — CAL packages, CML software, associated curriculum materials — was produced and tested with students. Details of this material are to be found in NDPCAL's *Program Index* (NDPCAL, 1977).

Conclusion

The recent severity of budgetary cuts in education and training has perhaps increased the validity of institutionalisation as a measure of educational acceptability. A success rate of 70% with institutionalisation, under these conditions, is felt to be very encouraging. However, too much store must not be put by claimed success rates with institutionalisation. There is always a possibility that the radical innovation will fail to be institutionalised because it requires too much reorganisation and rethinking, whereas the mundane and trivial application of the computer will be taken on.

There is evidence in some cases that, whilst CAL and CML may not get institutionalised, some of the accompanying 'multiple' innovations may. In the South Glamorgan CML project for the teaching of reading at primary school level, the computer component has disappeared leaving behind the likely adoption of a manual system of individualised, resource-based teaching. In Clwyd a network of history teachers involved

A CAL graphics package being demonstrated in a lecture

in local curriculum development, with or without the computer, is the heritage of NDPCAL funding.

References

CARNEGIE COMMISSION ON HIGHER EDUCATION (1972) *The Fourth Revolution — Instructional Technology in Higher Education*, New York: McGraw-Hill

MACDONALD, B, JENKINS, D, KEMMIS, S, and TAWNEY, D (1975) *The Programme at Two,* University of East Anglia: Centre for Applied Research in Education

NDPCAL (1977) *Project Summaries and Program Index*, London: National Development Programme in Computer Assisted Learning

2. Progress with transferability

Concern for transferability arose from the last three words of the main aim ' ... at reasonable cost'. For reasonable cost to be achieved, the high development costs of CAL and CML had to be shared amongst large numbers of users. Also, transferability, like institutionalisation, is another useful measure of educational value. The term 'transferability' was defined as the systematic attempt to promote the spread of experience, new ideas and teaching materials. For a review of the strategies used to encourage transferability see Chapter 6 in Part Three.

Figures 5 and 6 in the previous chapter, which set out the number of institutions and teaching staff involved in NDPCAL projects, would suggest that considerable transferability has been achieved. The experience of CAL and CML has become broadly distributed across the United Kingdom with primary centres of activity causing secondary 'infections'. From the beginning, the Programme set out to achieve this 'multiplier effect'.

The CALCHEM project, based at Leeds University and Sheffield City Polytechnic, began with 12 teachers in seven institutions, spreading to 91 teachers in 13 institutions. The Engineering Sciences Project (ESP), based at Queen Mary College, began with five teachers in five departments of engineering in three institutions, spreading to 40 teachers in 11 departments in seven institutions. At school level, the Hertfordshire maths project began in four schools spreading to 13 schools in the county and three schools in the Inner London Education Authority.

Two projects achieved secondary, and then tertiary, 'infections'. The CAMOL system, developed at the New University of Ulster for degree-level education courses, transferred successfully to Methodist College, Belfast for use in A-level physics. From Methodist College the CAMOL system plus the A-level physics course was transferring in the summer of 1977 to a group of schools in the Birmingham local education authority. The MATLAB system, developed at Napier College, Edinburgh, transferred to Paisley College at the beginning of the development project stage (DP 1/07), and Paisley then moved the materials into use in a few local schools, for example Paisley Grammar.

Towards the end of the Programme, a further wave of transfer events took place, to other institutions outside those directly involved with the projects. The other institutions' experience with the materials or ideas imported was almost impossible to evaluate. Follow-up questionnaires were not completed with any great regularity. By the summer of 1977, NDPCAL projects had transferred work to 125 other institutions in the UK and 12 other countries (see Figure 5). The CALCHEM project, for example, had transferred the teaching materials and the STAF author language facility to 12 institutions in four countries. The ESP project had transferred 18 different CAL packages to 28 institutions in eight countries.

Types of transferability

Complete transfer

The least usual method of transfer was the complete movement of a CAL package (computer program, documentation, students' and teachers' notes) or of a total CML system. At schools level and in further education, this is more likely to happen than in higher education. The biggest example of complete transfer in the Programme was the move of Broderick's SSRC-funded CML system including the biology course from the London Borough of Havering to schools in Lothian (TP 22/05). Despite problems with converting the computer software from ALGOL into FORTRAN (the focus of NDPCAL funding), pilot trials in Lothian in 1976/7 school year proved successful and plans were under way to develop further uses of the CML system particularly for in-service training of teachers. In 1977, Aberdeen and Dundee also purchased the CML system from Havering.

Part transfer

More usually, transfer of parts of a CAL package took place. For example, students' notes were rewritten by the importing institution. In the CALCHEM project, the computer programs were designed to be modular, so that different institutions took different parts — the theory sections not the simulated experiment, the data analysis section only, and so on. In the Programme's experience, ease of modification by the importing teacher or institution significantly increases chances of transfer being undertaken. The Leeds statistics project developed special control programs allowing teachers to construct their own individual combination of pre-written modules. The Birmingham geography project (CALUSG) developed teaching materials on the computer for use in secondary schools with *or without* access to a computer. By the end of 1976/7 the materials had been piloted in 11 schools in six local education authorities.

Ideas transfer

The transfer of ideas and experience became a central feature of the Programme's work. The Computers in the Undergraduate Science Curriculum project (CUSC), based at University College London, was highly successful at sharing experience, software standards and ideas amongst 60 academic staff in four institutions (UCL, Chelsea College, Surrey University and Queen Elizabeth College) and three disciplines (physics, biology and chemistry). Another example of ideas transfer was from higher education to military training. Both the University of Surrey and Queen Mary College were directly involved in encouraging CAL activity at officer-level institutions such as Shrivenham and Greenwich. In addition, Ken Knight of the University of Surrey was 'lent' to RAF Locking to help set up the SAFARI project (FS 3/03A). This transfer reduced the start-up time significantly, with a CAL system working with trainees on a new computer inside a year.

'Content-free' transfer

A particular transfer method that developed during the Programme concerned the use of 'content-free' software (a common set of computer programs that can be 'filled' with different contents to teach different subjects). The most dramatic example was the CAMOL project (Computer Assisted Management Of Learning), a collaborative venture between the Programme, International Computers Limited (ICL) and a group of education and training institutions. The CAMOL suite of programs provides a range of functions to manage learning, either in individualised systems or more conventional group-paced instruction. A central feature of CAMOL's design is modularity, allowing different users to use different parts, and also add local requirements. By the summer of 1977 CAMOL was coming into use, or already in use, in a university (New University of Ulster), two polytechnics (Brighton and Ulster), a further education college (Bradford), a group of secondary schools (Belfast and Birmingham), and the Royal Signals Technician Training School at Catterick Camp. The range of 'contents' covered by CAMOL is wide — school physics, craft-level mathematics, degree courses, military training.

Another example of 'content-free' transfer concerned the CAL group at the University of Glasgow. Case-study simulations, developed for teaching medical students, were successfully transferred for use — with different contents — in police training, and the in-service training of guidance counsellors.

Program exchanges

The Programme funded two program exchange/library projects, as the beginnings of an 'aftercare' structure for CAL following the Programme's end in 1977 (see Part Four). The Physical Sciences Program Exchange (PSPE) was already in operation before National Programme funds were injected. PSPE grew from a membership of eight institutions in 1974 (one overseas) to 66 institutions (23 overseas) in 1976/7. By 1976/7 the program library contained over 100 computer programs, which were being distributed at the rate of 13 a month. The Geographical Association Package Exchange (GAPE) was started by the National Programme. By the summer of 1977 it had 12 CAL packages in its library and 30 user institutions.

Conclusion

Somewhat ironically, the high development costs of CAL may *increase* with the need to make CAL transferable in order to spread those development costs. The teacher using CAL he has developed for himself does not, according to some projects, need the extensive documentation that is necessary for CAL materials to transfer. The CUSC project at its final review in May 1977 estimated that it might cost ten times as much to make a CAL package transferable as it does to make one for use by a teacher in his own course. The Engineering Sciences Project, on the other hand, held the view that the same standards of development and documentation should apply whether the package is 'internal' or 'external'. Investment in CAMOL by the National Programme, ICL and the cooperating institutions, totalled in all £600,000. It is difficult to be certain at what point investment in cheap special-purpose software for use in one context should give way to investment in expensive general-purpose software for use in many contexts.

The price tag for ensuring transferability is of particular importance looking towards the future. Given the way in which education and training institutions are budgeted, there are no obvious financial incentives to make software, which is working well locally, transferable. This is certainly true of institutions which are net exporters of CAL and CML. Whilst the Programme can claim to have achieved a very satisfactory level of success with institutionalisation and transferability, it did not begin to achieve the institutionalisation of transferability. This remains to be done in the post-1977 era.

PART TWO

THE EFFECTS AND COSTS OF COMPUTER ASSISTED LEARNING

The evidence of successful institutionalisation and transferability, set out in Part One, is a tangible measure of the educational value of computer assisted learning techniques. But it cannot be an entirely adequate measure, since educational innovations which are not considered worthwhile do get institutionalised. Part Two, therefore, contains summary reports from the two independent evaluation teams on the educational potential of computer assisted and computer managed learning, and on the costs. More detailed coverage of these topics, and evaluation of the Programme's overall strategy and performance, are to be found in the evaluators' own final reports.

3. Computer assisted learning: its educational potential

This chapter is written by Barry MacDonald, Roderick Atkin, David Jenkins and Stephen Kemmis of the Centre for Applied Research in Education, University of East Anglia. It reflects the work of the whole UNCAL (independent educational evaluation) team: the authors and David Tawney, Robert Stake, Gajendra Verma and Rob Walker. The reader should allow for some disparity of view within the group.

The aim of this chapter is to suggest ways we might assimilate our thinking about computer assisted learning into our thinking about educational processes and options more generally. What we have to suggest is based upon our experience of the National Programme, but our interest in what follows is in the potential contribution of the computer to education rather than in its current level of accomplishment. This, then, is less an evaluation of the performance of the National Programme than an attempt to say what has been learned about computer assisted learning through the medium of the Programme. As we write, the story of NDPCAL is still unfolding. The final UNCAL evaluation report is in preparation, with a view to publication in 1978.

Introduction

Those with long memories, who recall the revolutionary promise of educational television in the fifties, of teaching machines and programmed instruction in the sixties, may well be sceptical about the future of the computer in the classroom. Another 'machine', more 'programming', the technological error in yet another form. '*Plus ça change*' is the sceptic's weary response, we have been here before. And it doesn't help that much of the talk of the early innovators, being designed to persuade sponsors to disburse large sums of money for support, was inflated in educational terms, and imprudent in political terms. Teachers do not take kindly to the notion of their imminent dispensability, and it was not just classical scholars who were offended when one of the first books published in this country on the subject (Fine, 1962) claimed that the pioneering American electronic teacher PLATO was 'almost as intelligent as its namesake, the Plato of old'. Such claims did more than merely camouflage the gap between promise and performance: they misconstrued the nature of the promise itself. Like most innovations, computer assisted learning suffered heavily at the hands of its friends. And so, just as programmed instruction, in both book and machine form, has settled largely for a place in technician training, and television for distant learning within the Open University framework and for supplementing conventional classroom fare, might we not expect the computer in due course to assume an equally modest role in the teaching/learning environment?

It is important to state that, after closely observing the explorations in computer assisted learning promoted by the National Programme for the past four years, we do not incline to this view. Computers are here to stay in education, and will play an increasing role in the experience of learning. There are many reasons for taking this view, but we shall summarise just a few. The computer is as versatile a tool as the teaching machine was restricted. Its potential in education is virtually unknowable at this primitive stage but its ubiquity and importance in society at large ensures its continued technological development, which ensures in turn that its educational possibilities will continue to be explored. It is not tied to a particular view of how students learn, or how teachers should teach, so that its survival does not depend upon the stability of pedagogical theory. Finally, it is already clear that the machinery required to support computer assisted learning, the hardware itself, is rapidly becoming cheap and small without loss of capacity as the manufacturers move into the phase of mass production and miniaturisation.

The reader may wonder whether to deduce from this that we expect the computer to improve education. Here prophecy becomes hazardous, and not just because the reader's view of educational excellence may differ from ours. The computer is versatile; it may be used to teach facts, concepts, skills, imagination, to subjugate the learner or to emancipate him; it has a place in the pedagogies of instruction, discovery, and enquiry. The spread and diversity of applications is already wide, and each has its advocates and adversaries. Of course some applications will flourish and others will fade. But the mix of economic, administrative, professional and popular considerations which shape educational practice is too complex to support predictions of the forms of computer assisted learning that will be favoured. Our task is to state as clearly as possible what the options represent in terms of educational values, theories, justifications and issues. The reader will make his own judgements of merit.

The stereotype of CAL

It is important to realise the extent to which the National Programme represents a departure from a monolithic tradition of computer based curriculum development, a tradition, largely American, which has given rise to a stereotyped view of what computer assisted learning means. The stereotype conceives CAL as computerised programmed instruction which is used as a replacement for conventional teaching. The evaluation issue seems relatively straightforward; is CAI (computer assisted instruction — the American term associated with this view) more or less effective than what it replaces?

It is not difficult to understand why the stereotype is so strong, or why the evaluation issue associated with it is equally persistent. The predominant emphasis in the first decade of the new learning technology (1960-1970) was on this type of utilisation, with the computer restricted to a tutorial or exerciser role. And the near exclusive emphasis of evaluation studies has been on comparative experiments designed to determine whether or not computerised provision was a better way of teaching the same things.

None of us can be sure about what kinds of computer based learning will characterise the next decade, but it is worth noting influential reactions to this tradition. The Carnegie Commission on Higher Education, in its latest report, (Rockhart and Scott Morton, 1975), concludes that

'CAI has been overemphasised. In the areas of learning where it is applicable, other technologies dominate along the relevant dimensions . . . The primary clear target of opportunity for the computer in Higher Education is in "enrichment activities". For almost all kinds of material, problem solving, games and simulation can provide the learner with better ways of integrating and testing the knowledge he has acquired than other available technologies . . . It follows that the impact of CAL will for the most part be adding to rather than replacing current learning mechanisms.'

The Commission argues (albeit with perhaps too much faith in the survival of the most fitting) that CAI, at its best, is insufficiently superior to alternative technologies to justify its continued dominance in the field of computer assisted learning. Although confined to the higher education sector, this argument is consistent with the findings of the most authoritative review of CAI in schools, that of Jamison, Suppes and Wells (1974). Summarising all the available evaluation studies, overwhelmingly of the controlled comparison type based on achievement scores, they conclude that CAI is no more than equally effective as an alternative to traditional instruction.

Because of the dominance of CAI, and perhaps because of its susceptibility to experimental/control group comparisons, there have been few attempts to assess the effects on learning of computer based approaches which do not fall within the CAI bracket. The Carnegie Commission thought it might be four or five years before evidence of the effectiveness of 'enrichment' applications became available.

When we turn to the National Programme and look at the pattern of use across the projects we can immediately see the extent to which the Programme has anticipated the Carnegie Commission's recommendations in terms of its development targets. The Programme has sponsored a portfolio of applications of considerable diversity, but with an overall emphasis on types of applications which CAI has neglected.

The Programme has not, however, escaped the legacy of the CAI controversy which, particularly in the early stages of NDPCAL, played a rhetorically strong role in debates between Programme participants with regard to tutorial applications. In the end the debate has shown nothing so much as that the opposition between CAL and CAI is an oversimplification of alternative pedagogies within the Programme — one looks in vain for 'pure' examples of mechanistic (page-turning programmed learning) CAI; and its alleged alternative, imaginative CAL, is a highly differentiated collection of uses of the computer. The CALCHEM project, for instance, reveals the complexity in the way it defines its tutorial approach: 'enhanced tutorial programs provide a number of alternative dialogues, the routing through which may be determined by the student's current and previous responses, and which may make use of facilities for simulation, calculation, graph plotting, etc, within the tutorial sequence' (Ayscough, 1977).

Another convenient example is that of the Leeds statistics project. This project grew out of an SSRC research project carried out by the Computer Based Learning Project at Leeds University, perhaps the most stable centre of CAL research and development in the National Programme. Its work covers a range of CAL applications from adaptive-tutorial CAL to artificial intelligence (AI) work with Seymour Papert's LOGO system, as well as problems of knowledge acquisition and language comprehension. The NDPCAL-sponsored statistics work of the Project is clearly adaptive-tutorial in character but, unlike 'doctrinaire' CAI, it is not conceived as a self-instructional replacement for a conventional social sciences statistics course. Such use of the materials is regarded by the Project as 'sub-optimal': ideally, the CAL work supports and deepens students' understandings by providing opportunities for practice and guided problem-solving in statistics.

To characterise and evaluate even the Programme portfolio requires that we move outside the assumptions of CAI thinking and try to bring to bear on the CAL experience that wider range of educational perspectives which seems to have guided its various practices. In the section which follows we suggest three analytic frameworks (paradigms) within which CAL can be understood, and discuss the possible emergence of a fourth. We hope that the example of CALCHEM will serve to remind the reader of the dangers of polarising and stereotyping project work through a rigid application of these frameworks. Computer managed learning (CML) and computer assisted training (CAT) are discussed in subsequent sections of the chapter.

Educational paradigms for CAL

The National Programme has spawned some thirty-five projects and studies involving the computer in educational and training processes. To understand them adequately, each has to be studied in its own terms and circumstances. Summarising across their diversity is a difficult, even dangerous business, but it is the business of this chapter, and we propose to begin it by proposing three paradigms of education through which we may grasp the major ways in which the developers of computer assisted learning conceive the curriculum task. We have called these paradigms the 'instructional', the 'revelatory' and the 'conjectural', although the labels themselves may be less helpful than the profiles which they summarise. It should be emphasised that few of the projects which we allocate to these paradigms explicitly call them forth in explaining and justifying their work; they are our 'inventions', intended to help the reader relate CAL to the general field of educational theory and practice.

The instructional paradigm

This paradigm is strongly associated with classic drill-and-practice programs of American CAI, and with adaptive-tutorial projects in NDPCAL. Much of the work of the Glasgow mathematics, CALCHEM, Leeds statistics, and Post Office technician training projects falls within this paradigm. The theory was at one time derived from Skinner's doctrine of operant conditioning based on the reinforcement of successful responses and the atomisation of complex tasks, moved through an 'instructional psychology' phase which drew its support from theorists like Gagné and Glaser, and has more recently taken up theoretical trends concerned with knowledge acquisition and language comprehension (eg Freedle and Carroll). In general, the instructional paradigm involves the belief that the knowledge students need to acquire can be specified in language and learned by the transmission and reception of verbal messages.

Key concept: mastery of content.

Curriculum emphasis: subject matter as the object of learning.

Educational means: rationalisation of instruction, especially in terms of sequencing presentation and feedback reinforcement.

Role of the computer: presentation of content, task prescription, student motivation through fast feedback.

Assumptions: conventional body of subject matter with articulated structure; articulated hierarchy of tasks; behaviouristic learning theory.

Idealisation/caricature: at best, the computer is seen as a patient tutor; at worst it is seen as a page turner.

NDPCAL project closest to the paradigm: Glasgow mathematics, which has the linear characteristics of traditional programmed learning.

The revelatory paradigm

Simulation and some kinds of data-handling programs are rooted in this paradigm. Within the National Programme, projects such as CUSC, Glasgow medicine, the Engineering Sciences Project and the RNC Greenwich project can usefully be looked at within this framework. In terms of the underlying educational psychology, theorists such as Bruner (the spiral curriculum) and perhaps Ausubel (subsumption theory) would be most supportive. Typically, the view of learning emphasises closing the gap between the structure of the student's knowledge and the structure of the discipline he is trying to master. It could be labelled the 'conceptual' paradigm because of the importance attached to the key ideas of established knowledge fields. We call it 'revelatory' because these key ideas are more or less gradually 'revealed' to the learner.

Key concept: discovery, intuition, getting a 'feel' for ideas in the field, etc.

Curriculum emphasis: the student as the subject of education.

Educational means: provision of opportunities for discovery and vicarious experience.

Role of computer: simulation or information-handling.

Assumptions: (hidden) model of significant concepts and knowledge structure; theory of learning by discovery.

Idealisation/caricature: at best, the computer is seen as creating a rich learning environment; at worst, it makes a 'black box' of the significant learnings.

NDPCAL project closest to the paradigm: CUSC (Computers in the Undergraduate Science Curriculum) which attempts through simulation to make complex ideas accessible to students. Each simulation package is built around a mathematical model of a physical system; as the student manipulates it, he is expected to develop an intuitive understanding of the model. This understanding helps him to appreciate the theoretical formalisation of the model.

The conjectural paradigm
This paradigm may be appropriate for modelling and artificial intelligence packages and for computer science applications. An assortment of NDPCAL projects including CPTL (Computational Physics Teaching Laboratory) at Surrey University, the Programme-related work at the Cambridge University Department of Applied Mathematics and Theoretical Physics, and the London Business School Management Decision Making Project, fall within it, although in each case many of the important student experiences take place away from the computer. People who operate within this paradigm tend towards the view that knowledge is created through experience and evolves as a psychological and social process. Authoritative theorists of this persuasion are Piaget (adaptation through interaction with the environment), Popper

(conjectures and refutations), and, within computer learning theory itself, Papert.

Key concept: articulation and manipulation of ideas and hypothesis-testing.

Curriculum emphasis: understanding, 'active' knowledge.

Educational means: manipulation of student inputs, finding metaphors and model building.

Role of computer: manipulable space/field/'scratch-pad'/language, for creating or articulating models, programs, plans or conceptual structures.

Assumptions: problem-oriented theory of knowledge; general cognitive theory.

Idealisation/caricature: at best, the computer is seen as a tool or educational medium (in the sense of milieu, *not* 'communications medium'), at worst, as an expensive toy.

NDPCAL-related project closest to the paradigm: Cambridge DAMTP (Department of Applied Mathematics and Theoretical Physics) where the use of the computer as an alternative to analytic methods simplifies the process of mathematical investigation, allowing students to construct models of physical systems and test the assumptions of the models by computing their consequences.

Learning, labour and emancipation — a fourth paradigm?

Although the precise terminology we have used in delineating the three paradigms may be somewhat idiosyncratic, the style and broad content will be familiar enough to students of education, and will, we hope, give a grip on the CAL field. They may, however, by emphasising those attributes of CAL which it shares with other educational practices, miss some important issues, and we wish at this point to explore a perspective on CAL which takes as its starting point an aspect of the computer which is held to be its most important characteristic in applications outside education, namely its power as a labour-saving facility.

It is possible to conceptualise the activities of students (and of teachers) as 'labour' and therefore to consider how CAL as a labour-saving device, affects their work. To do this it is helpful to distinguish between authentic labour (valued learning), and inauthentic labour (activities which may be instrumental to valued learning, but are not valued for their own sake). The justification of some forms of CAL is that it enhances authentic labour, for others that it reduces inauthentic labour. Much curriculum reform and development is of the first kind: making difficult ideas more accessible, making learning more 'relevant', or more fully engaging students' own interests. Examples of CAL which attempt to enhance the authenticity of the learning experience include CUSC simulations (as in the Schroedinger equation package which allows students to interact with the model and thus to learn its characteristics), the Glasgow Clinical Decision-Making Project's packages (which give students a 'feel' for the problems of diagnosis and patient management normally only achieved in clinical work) and CPTL (where students learn to write programs to solve physical problems).

The three paradigms we have already outlined are generally compatible with the idea of enhancing the authenticity of student labour. The instructional paradigm does so by leading the student through a body of subject-matter in a rationally organised way, the revelatory by bringing the student to the 'heart' of a problem and helping him to feel its significance, and the conjectural by allowing the student to explore the ramifications of his own ideas.

The computer is peculiarly suited to reducing the amount of inauthentic student labour, however, and many CAL applications exploit the information-handling capacities of the computer to improve the quality of the learning experience by taking the tedium out of some kinds of tasks.

The idea of using CAL for this purpose suggests the possibility of a fourth paradigm, one which is yet unarticulated in detail. It is by no means as coherent as the three primary paradigms; perhaps it is a kind of inverse image which can appear in association with any of the others. This fourth paradigm we have called *emancipatory*. In so far as it has any coherence, its key concept is the notion of reducing the inauthenticity of student labour. Its curriculum emphasis and educational means are derived from the primary paradigm with which it is associated — for it never appears in isolation except as an impulse to curriculum reform. The role of the computer is calculation, graph-plotting, tabulation or other information handling. Examples of this emancipatory paradigm in CAL include Napier's MATLAB project (where the computer is used to carry out otherwise tedious calculations and where the curriculum reform is of a revelatory kind, emphasising mathematical concepts rather than techniques), the Suffolk Local History Classroom Project (where the computer tabulates census data for the pupils and where the curriculum reform is conjectural, emphasising history as hypothesis-testing and the use of evidence), the Imperial College CAL work on fluid flow and heat transfer (a part of the Engineering Sciences Project — ESP; where the computer allows numerical solutions to be found for real-life problems which are analytically intractable, and where the curriculum reform is more revelatory, elaborating the notions of fluid flow and heat transfer in more complex and industrially interesting situations), and some of the CALCHEM work (where the computer reduces the inauthenticity of the learning situation by plotting graphs or carrying out calculations for students as a separate but complementary role to its enhancement of the authenticity of the learning experience in tutorial CAL). The work of the CALUSG project in geography which produces difficult-to-generate quantitative data for classroom use might also be considered emancipatory but is as much a saving of labour for the teacher as for the student.

Whether or not we wish to dignify this emancipatory interest of curriculum reform with the label 'paradigm' there can be no doubt that it is a compelling impulse. The 'information explosion' has emphasised the problem for teachers of how to reduce the complexity of subject-matter for students and has posed the companion problem of finding criteria by which the reduction can be justified. Common criteria for justifying the inclusion of a topic in the curriculum are its significance (to teachers or other subject matter authorities) and the utility of the information (to students or their prospective employers). The potential of CAL as a labour-saving device which can reduce the amount of time students spend (or, rather, waste) in inauthentic labour may thus be welcomed by teachers as a way of easing the complexity problem. As many have argued for the hand calculator, CAL may divert students from tasks not valuable in themselves (and which are understood in principle) to other, more highly valued activities.

These three or four paradigms are essentially ways of thinking about the *curriculum* tasks faced by the CAL developers. We have discussed them in terms of the place of computer-based education in the wider environments of teaching and learning, and it is not surprising therefore that they reflect the aspirations and educational values held by their developers. But how CAL can realise these aspirations is a separate question, and one which poses major research and evaluation questions. It is to these questions that we now turn.

Student learning: a CAL typology

The main research question to be faced in considering the educational value of CAL concerns the nature of learning itself. In what language can the educational processes and learning outcomes be discussed? This section attempts to gain purchase on the issue by developing a typology of student-CAL interactions. The reason for this line of attack is straightforward — it is in the process of *interaction* (learning in a CAL environment) that the promises for an effective computer-related pedagogy are delivered or denied. Using the typology it is possible to describe, virtually on a moment-by-moment basis, the process of computer assisted learning.

As we indicated earlier, in discussing American CAI, the tradition of student learning evaluation in CAL is an arid one which has yielded little understanding of the distinctive nature of the learning experience. As evaluators of the NDPCAL we decided to turn our attention from tests of attainment to the processes of learning. This is partly because such tests will be equivocal about the merits of CAL, partly because they will rarely have been constructed so that they are valid tests of the particular kind of learning the CAL experience promotes. To get to the heart of the issue, we dispensed with the notion of providing an actuarial summary of achievement and instead focused our attention on the CAL experience itself, attempting to formulate a scheme within which the kind of learning which goes on when the student and the CAL technology come into contact can be described. In this way, we reasoned, it might be possible to define the educational potential of CAL whether tests used to assess student attainment are valid or not.

To achieve this, we have developed a typology of student-CAL interactions (Kemmis, 1976). The 'types' themselves are derived on the one hand from the research literature on learning, and on the other from the claims made in justification of CAL. The literature provides ways of thinking about the nature of learning, while the claims of CAL developers yield insights into the values by which CAL may be judged. And it is in the processes of interaction in CAL environments that promises of education are fulfilled or frustrated.

Each of the following five 'types' refers to the interactions between the student and the immediate CAL context. What distinguishes the types is the kinds of opportunities they offer for learning, and what the typology does is to make explicit the kind of learning that might be claimed on the basis of specific student interactions with the CAL technology.

Type A: recognition

In the case of recognition-type interactions, the student is merely required to indicate whether or not the information presented by the machine, in the form of a question or incomplete statement, has been presented previously.

Multiple choice or binary choice (yes/no) items occurring in CAL interactions are sometimes of this type. We have found no significant examples of Type A in the National Programme.

Type B: recall

Recall-type interactions require the student to do more than recognise information presented, but they do not call for understanding. They require the student to reproduce textual information in either verbatim or transformed verbatim (rearranged syntactically or logically, but not in terms of meaning) forms.

Recitation, sentence completion and cloze-type test items exemplify verbatim recall interactions; some kinds of sentence completion, free recall, matching, and some kinds of low-level logical inference questions, exemplify transformed verbatim interactions.

Example: from an (atypical) CUSC package — note that this interaction takes place via a VDU (visual display unit) terminal. The text disappears from the screen before the question appears; question and answer are displayed together.

Text: The spin QN of an electron can take two values: $+\frac{1}{2}$ and $-\frac{1}{2}$.

Question: What are the two values of the spin QN?

Answer: $+\frac{1}{2}$, $-\frac{1}{2}$.

Type B interactions involve only a superficial engagement of the student with the material; within the National Programme, they do not feature frequently and seem to occur only in tutorial modes in higher education and in technician training.

Type C: reconstructive understanding or comprehension

This kind of interaction is by far the most pervasive in the CAL materials produced under the sponsorship of the National Programme, ranging from some quite elementary types of comprehension to some fairly subtle ones. These types of interaction do not depend on the superficial features of the information presented as with Types A and B; rather, they engage the student in meaningful operations on the content presented. He may be called upon to reconstruct statements, concepts, or principles, but this will generally be within the limits of what has been presented; the boundaries of what is learned will always be more or less clearly determined by the semantic content of the information given in the interaction. The following example (again from CUSC) illustrates a Type C interaction calling for the understanding of a principle.

Example

Question: How many planar nodes are there in the wave function of a 7D electron?

Answer: 2

Our comment: To answer this question, the student must make a new inference on the basis of a simple principle and a statement. He must apply the principle in the stated case to answer the question. He knows from previous learning that $l =$ number of planar nodes, and that the value of l for a D electron is 2. So he can deduce that a 7D electron has 2 planar nodes.

Type D: global reconstructive or intuitive understanding

These interactions are much more difficult to describe. They often involve prolonged activity and are directed at 'getting a feel' for an idea, developing sophisticated pattern-recognition skills, or a sense of strategy.

The emphasis is on experiential learning which might develop an awareness by the student of his actions in the context of a constellation of problems or ideas recognised by experts as critical to understanding a field of knowledge. Here, more than in Types A, B and C, understanding must be demonstrated in what the student *does*, and it will be judged accordingly by teachers. (It cannot be judged by explicit criteria stored in the machine).

Type D CAL interactions involve such activities as discovering principles behind simulations, developing a 'feel' for diagnostic strategies, problem-solving using classical techniques, and the like. Type D interactions are common to all sectors of the National Programme with the exception of technician training.

Take for example, the emergency simulation packages of the Glasgow medical project. Learning the diagnostic strategies of the expert physician takes place through Type D interactions, where the student tries out courses of action in the form of alternative tests and treatments. The aspiration is to develop the clinician's sense of the appropriateness of different courses of action in different contexts.

Type E: constructive understanding

Type E interactions are extremely open-ended and involve the student in 'creating' knowledge. Because the creation of new knowledge almost always takes place against a context of old knowledge, Type E interactions are usually intertwined with other kinds, especially Type D. Because of the type of use of the machine in Type E interactions, however, the learning process may be taking place away from the terminal. In Type E interactions, the student engages in 'open' enquiry: he is not working towards solutions which are necessarily within the known structure of the discipline. From his point of view he is going beyond what is known. He may be testing his own hypotheses, developing his own methodologies and drawing conclusions based on his own work. Type E interactions look like genuine research, not just exercises on the content and methods of fields already known. Examples of Type E within the National Programme can be found in higher education (although Types C and D are more common there), in management education, and in the use of data bases in the schools sector. In the last case, a pupil in the history class interrogates a data base to explicate and to test hypotheses about the conditions of life of nineteenth-century agricultural labourers. In part, his work conforms to what is already known about nineteenth-century rural industry and the methods of professional historians (which look like Type D interactions though they are not student-CAL but student-teacher or student-print interactions), but he is writing new history himself, not just learning what others have discovered.

The paradigms and the typology

Readers may wonder why we have offered two analytic schemes (the paradigms and the typology) where perhaps one might have served. The answer is that the two schemes address different levels of discourse about CAL, the first being about curriculum and the second about learning processes. Discussion about CAL, we have found, take place at both levels, so that discussion of what teachers want to do is likely to take place at the curriculum (paradigm) level, while discussion about what teachers want students to learn is likely to take place at the learning-process

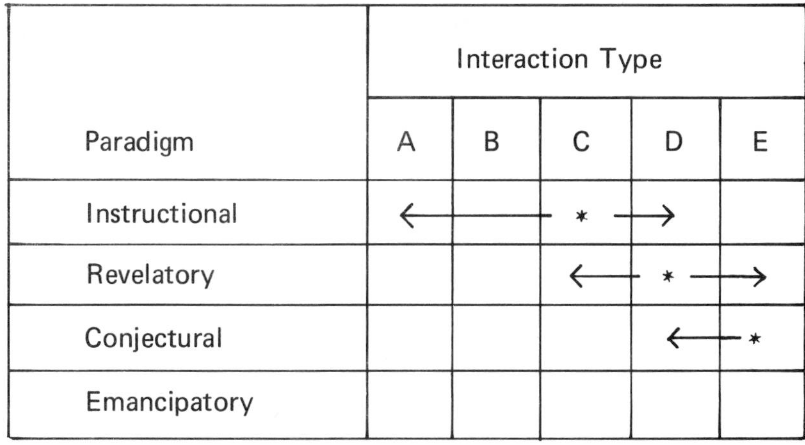

Paradigm	Interaction Type				
	A	B	C	D	E
Instructional	←	—	*	→	
Revelatory			←	*	→
Conjectural				←	*
Emancipatory					

Figure 7. Possible relations between paradigms and interaction types

(typology) level. As might be expected, the two levels overlap to some extent. Although each paradigm will in practice create opportunities for a range of types of interactions, critical interactions within the instructional paradigm are likely to be of Type C, within the relevatory paradigm, Type D, and within the conjectural paradigm, Type E. The emancipatory paradigm will not be exclusively associated with any particular type of interaction. Figure 7, though an oversimplification, summarises these relationships. A final note of caution might be added before we leave this schematic overview of CAL. The schemes themselves, merely by ordering curricular and learning-process perspectives on CAL, may appear to offer guarantees of its educational worthwhileness. It would be a mistake to draw such a conclusion. They are more appropriately seen as indicating kinds of *potential*. Actual achievement is a separate issue.

Realising the potential: a cautionary note

We have consistently emphasised the potential of CAL within the several paradigms, but we do not mean to leave the impression that this potential is readily fulfilled. Indeed, every project in the Programme has run into problems: some major, some trivial; some practical, some theoretical; some organisational, some human, some technical. It could be said — and we say it kindly, not to denigrate the work of project personnel — that every project has found new ways to fail. Because of the risk of singling out particular projects' work for attention, we would prefer to treat shortfalls in achievement by reference to our paradigms rather than the projects' own aims. They are intended only to illustrate the kinds of difficulties which arise whenever curriculum developers attempt to transmute curricular aspirations into educational practice.

Instructional: in the National Programme, one can find examples of 'adaptive-tutorial' CAL which require more adaptation of the student to the machine pedagogy than of the pedagogy to the learner. Even where the adaptive-tutorial materials are multi-branching, the student will usually follow a path through the subject-matter designed for him by the developer; even where a range of alternative responses is catered for by the machine, the materials impose their developers' questions and their developers' logic. Unlike advanced artificial intelligence (AI) applications in education (for example, Carbonell's SCHOLAR system), adaptive-tutorial CAL is unlikely to allow the student to pose his own questions or follow lines of his own interest. And student interest is important in the justification of instructional CAL: motivation based on feedback reinforcement may be insufficient in keeping the student engaged in his interaction with the machine.

Revelatory: in one project, we have seen examples of packages in which students have a dialogue with the machine intended to help them in planning experiments. The machine asks a variety of critical questions which guide the students towards a choice of methods and equipment for studying a phenomenon. But the difficulty is that students working on one experiment in the lab are nearly always exposed to other students who are working on other experiments. Since it is practically impossible to seal students off from one another, the social experience of the laboratory will thus tend to pre-empt the planning packages: the students will have seen how to do the experiment before they arrive at the terminals. They are in a position to 'outguess' the machine as it takes them through the planning process.

There are other kinds of difficulties, too, in teaching for 'revelation' — sometimes what is revealed turns out to be an oversimplified version of a complex judgement process, or a black-and-white version of a grey area of human judgement. Medical students working on patient management case studies, for example, may be presented with diagnosis or treatment options (laid out as if there were no problems of construing the patient's state in terms of options) and have their responses judged by reference to a 'consensus' of expert opinion. At one level, we may speak of the process as one of revelation — revealing expert clinicians' models of practice. At another level, we may see the process as one of subjugation — what is revealed to the student is an apparent consensus among clinicians (who, in fact, disagree about all but the most proper and improper courses of action).

Conjectural: perhaps the biggest difficulty in practice within the conjectural paradigm is that of developing students to the point where the machine becomes a 'mere' tool for the pursuit of other learning. On the one hand, there is the problem of helping computer-naive students to use the machine as a 'scratch-pad' when the ideas they are pursuing are themselves complex and subtle; on the other hand, there is the problem of helping them, after they have reached this mastery of the machine as a tool, to free themselves from the categories it imposes on the way they think about the problems. In one project, for example, the machine imposes the categories of 'concept' and 'element' for purposes of thinking about managers' perspectives on management problems — once the machine has introduced the separation, which it uses to make apparent certain kinds of interrelations between ideas and their objects, it may be difficult for students to think otherwise about perspectives.

Emancipatory: using the computer to take the tedium out of calculations may have paradoxical consequences. In some settings, students have traditionally regarded 'doing the problems' as both the experience and the evidence of learning: they see the calculation as being the problem. When a project changes the nature of the problem so that it becomes, for example, seeing the significance of a mathematical model used in a number of relatively standard situations, the students may act so as to conserve their traditional ways of thinking. They may 'subvert' the new approach, treating the computer as a generator of numerical solutions and report that they have not learned anything from the CAL exercise. Taking inauthentic labour out of the learning process thus does not guarantee that authentic learning will be enhanced — that, too, must be achieved.

Freeing the student from one kind of non-valued activity, however, may still leave problems: sometimes the process of using the machine is sufficiently difficult that students must expend as much energy in using the machine to get solutions as they would in doing the calculations.

General: in addition to these paradigm-related difficulties there are more general pitfalls awaiting the unwary CAL developer. We have observed machines that were inherently or acutely unreliable, teachers who found difficulty explaining to students what CAL materials were intended to do, problems of sequencing CAL materials within the general stream of course experiences, materials that underestimated the complexity or the subtlety of the ideas they attempted to convey, the professed ideal of the patient tutor in some CAL rendered as pedantry, packages so subtle that they defied penetration by students without additional guidance, CAL-related curricular innovations so far-reaching in their implications that they defied implementation except in diluted forms, student-terminal interface software so complex as to demand a kind of 'translation' of communication with the machine into and out of the language in which the subject-matter is usually discussed, and, even in an emphatically teacher-led programme, the occasional dominance of computer technologists over teachers in the design of CAL materials.

As in all curriculum development, CAL developers in the National Programme are learning by their mistakes. Though these remarks may have alerted the reader to some of the ways it is possible to fail, many CAL developers in the National Programme would argue that it is only by doing, and by making mistakes, that it is possible to gain a practical grasp of the problems of CAL development.

Computer managed learning

When we turn to what has been termed computer managed learning (CML) we find that the role played by the computer is relatively indirect. Students do not work at a terminal, as they do in CAL, but take part in courses of study in which some of the management tasks have been taken over by the machine. This distinction is significant enough in terms of educational applications to warrant separate treatment, even a separate analytical framework, which we now propose.

The managerial paradigm

All computer managed learning applications belong within this paradigm. Its theoretical origins are obscure, and probably lie outside education, in management science and systems engineering. Within education, it derives support from educational technology generally, from such theorists as Bloom (mastery learning) and Glaser (criterion-referenced testing and psycho/technological approaches to learning). In practice, its view of the nature of knowledge typically (though not exclusively) approximates to the 'instructional' view.

Key concept: optimisation of the teaching/learning process.

Curriculum emphasis: teacher or machine as manager of learning.

Educational means: rationalisation of needs/resource matching to improve efficiency of learning for the student.

Role of the computer: optimisation of the learner's route through a content field on the basis of his personality, cognitive characteristics, and diagnosed state of readiness.

Assumptions: modularised curriculum; theory of learning styles, student needs and aptitudes.

Idealisation/caricature: at best, CML is seen as capitalising on individual learner differences (in needs, cognitive styles, etc); at worst, it is held to be unnecessary (can be anticipated by teachers or students).

NDPCAL project closest to the paradigm: the South Glamorgan Remedial Reading scheme, which attempted (though it failed) to develop an operational system which would use a combination of previous performance and profiles of pupil characteristics to prescribe tasks for the learner.

Although CML shades across into mass applications of computers in educational administration (the sloughing off of routine clerical tasks to the machine), of more pressing educational interest are the three 'roles' played by the computer in CML systems: testing, routing students through courses of study, and record keeping.

Like CAL, CML is in principle responsive to alternative views of teaching and learning. It does not force the educator to make assumptions of a pedagogically committing kind. Nevertheless there is always a question that might reasonably be posed of any CML system: how does it envisage the interface between the human educators and the supportive machine? Particular CML systems might appear overtly mechanistic (ie inflexibly rule-bound) depending on what tasks, construed in what way, are handed over to the machine. The educational assumptions underpinning CML schemes are not in any simple sense packaged into the technology.

The source of demand for CML is frequently said to come from those who wish to individualise learning. Yet the desire to individualise learning itself contains two contradictory impulses. A liberal view might be constructed in terms of allowing more student autonomy. John Cowan in a paper to the 1976 APLET conference identified a 'hierarchy of freedoms related to learning'. The lowest freedom is freedom of pace, then freedom of method, freedom of content and freedom of assessment. Due to the hierarchical structure, offering one freedom implies offering all lower freedoms. The machine is said to match the intuitive adaptivity of the teacher and meet the claims made upon the instructional system by individual students. But paradoxically CML is also endorsed by those who support the thrust towards a tighter instructional system, based on pre-course or pre-module testing and mastery learning. It is quite possible for a single institution to use CML in both ways. At the New University of Ulster, for example, a 'liberal' (and even at times conjectural) application of CAMOL is found in Harry McMahon's course, ED204 Curriculum Design and Development, and a 'tight' application is found in Tom Black's course, DE380 Research Design and Structure, an off-shoot of the same project.

It may be useful to consider in turn the three principal roles played by the computer in CML systems, testing, routing and record-keeping.

Testing

The testing role means test marking, test analysis, test item banking and test production (not necessarily limited to formal examinations). It must be obvious that CML requires teachers to understand fully the role of testing in the educative setting. Not all tests, for example, are designed to discriminate between, or 'spread out' a group of students, and CML systems increasingly show the influence of mastery learning and criterion-referenced testing. Yet many teachers are unprepared technically for the sophistication of facilities offered by current CML systems. In the early days this was a problem in the CAMOL application at Brighton Polytechnic, for example. If one took an incremental view of educational innovation it would perhaps be sufficient to claim that the testing facilities offered to tutors in an imported CML innovation would be at least as good, even if imperfectly understood, as those they could generate themselves. CML testing typically increases the amount of information available to tutors, being greater than they could produce manually.

One form of testing prevalent in CML systems is diagnostic testing. In a 'tight' CML system, diagnostic testing will be based on a somewhat mechanistic assumption — that it is possible to generate decision rules by which learners move from supposedly diagnostic scores or profile characteristics to supposedly appropriate learning materials, having one-to-one correspondence with gaps in the learner's performance repertoire. But diagnostic testing might also be construed more loosely, as background data for making information-based educational judgements about what the students should do next.

Experience with the computer generation of test items is limited. Even when manually generated, it is rare for instructional materials to be rich enough to yield a large number of items. This will be particularly true of courses still under development and in a state of flux. Indeed it might well be argued that the investment of time and effort in building up items depends on the stability of the instructional materials.

Another problem is that objective testing, favoured by CML because it facilitates machine-marking, is frequently unsatisfactory vis-à-vis the way in which an expert understands the subject. Typically, multiple choice questions reward 'surface knowledge' at the expense of 'depth understanding', which may best be tested by demanding a constructed response. It would not be possible, for example, to infer mathematical understanding of a topic from a pupil's successful completion of machine marked questions in the Hertfordshire Computer Managed Maths Project.

Routing

The second role performed by the computer in CML systems is prescriptive, routing students through a course of study on the basis of past attainment and/or individual characteristics and interests. 'Routing' occurs when the machine designates paths to individual learners through learning materials. A typical approach to routing involves dividing a course up into a series of chunky modules or 'blocks'. Students only take those modules to which they are directed. But the claims for CML routing go beyond simple feed-forward systems involving prerequisites, mastery testing and remedial support. They quickly add up to statements about how this learner with these characteristics should learn within this domain. Consequently machine routing implies that we adequately understand the subject matter, and thus can represent the knowledge structure in some way; that we adequately characterise the learner to whose individual needs we claim to be adaptive; and that we adequately conceptualise a pedagogy.

Although at first sight the question of finding ways to represent knowledge might not seem a problem, Michael MacDonald Ross (1972) has pointed out that this is 'a real issue whose clarification is almost a prerequisite for progress in the design of educational systems'. One promising technical approach, the so-called behavioural objectives approach, no longer commands universal support, not least because it misrepresents knowledge as a 'list structure' ('it is the interconnectedness of ideas that makes knowledge coherent and this aspect is omitted by any protocol of behaviour', Ross, 1972). Alternative forms for representing knowledge include the hierarchy (in which knowledge is represented as a tree, with everything dependent on what is taught previously) and the relational net (which is rather like the map of the London Underground in that many routes are possible). But in each case the visual metaphor imposes a way of looking at the domain of learning that may or may not be helpful. Is the hierarchy logically necessary or just pedagogically expedient, the choice of a particular instructor? Should the nodes on a network be concepts or learning tasks? There is also the question of consistency. It is possible to find, as in the Havering biology scheme, a testing system premised on a list structure and a routing system premised on a hierarchy or network.

Without an adequate pedagogy for a CML course, judgement on the appropriateness of particular learning materials cannot be made. Yet CML systems are also being pressed to accommodate alternative learning styles, student preferences and variations in the mode of instruction.

There is a parallel between adaptive-tutorial CAL and CML routing. Both have attracted strong arguments within what we have called an instructional paradigm, asserting the right of the developer to design paths for the student, and build these in preordinately, ie, prior to the educational encounter. This strong claim insists that branches or routing algorithms can be established in advance, rendering unnecessary any further intuitive adaptivity on the part of the teacher. Such CML routing will tend to be mechanistic and prescriptive. Paradoxically, since CML is often justified in terms of the individualisation of learning, such routing may actually detract from any real individualisation. As David Hawkridge (1974) points out, the basic problem in using the computer to determine the sequence each learner should follow is one of finding reasons for reducing the options open to students at each decision point.

Another interesting aspect of CML routing, which directly affects the 'authority of the system' is whether students are expected to treat the machine and its advice as a mysterious 'black box', in principle closed to them. An alternative is to give students a map of the knowledge domain independent of the 'next step' instruction issued by the machine (the difference might be seen as similar to offering a driver a map of Cornwall rather than an AA Saltash-to-Bodmin route map) and permit browsing through the curriculum material. This would have the predictable consequence of legitimising the exercise of ordinary judgement as an alternative to accepting the routing suggested by the machine.

Record-keeping

Finally we need to consider the role of the computer in record-keeping. This is clearly important but intellectually unexciting, at best where economies of scale are possible over vast quantities of routinely collected data. Because of the facilities for analysis available in computers, the possibility of tailoring records of student progress (ranging in scale from the individual module to the whole course) to the information needs of different parties becomes a task of imaginative complexity. It is in this light that Ulster College sees its development of 'macro' CAMOL.

Conclusion

The educational justification for CML will always depend on identifying its goals as desirable and placing a value greater than cost on the differences between the CML system and what it replaces. Part of the justification is that the machine 'frees' teachers for a more personal educational role, what in terms of our analysis might be described as reducing the inauthentic labour of the *teacher*.

Computer assisted training

We have less to say about the role of the computer in industrial training, partly because our own experience and expertise lies more in the field of education and partly because the National Programme explorations in this sector have been limited, as the Director points out elsewhere. Our remarks, therefore, should be treated as speculative and thinly grounded.

Of course, the National Programme has indirectly covered a wider area than is shown by its two designated industrial training projects. The Leeds statistics work has clear application in a number of vocations. The Glasgow Clinical Decision-Making Project provides vocational training to doctors, and more recently, through transfer of the model, to police officers. And at Leicester Polytechnic, within the Engineering Sciences

Project, the visitor may meet day-release HND students from that same Post Office which elsewhere accommodates a project in industrial training.

This leads us to the difficult distinction between education and training, which, though useful, becomes increasingly blurred with the current emphasis on the industrial relevance of education. But the conventional distinction largely holds in some important respects. Training is job specific, and represents an investment in work force competence by employers demanding tangible evidence of enhanced performance. The dominant paradigms are instructional and managerial, with a strong flavour of systems theory. The modern industrial trainer operates through a process of segmenting the learning experience into carefully defined increments. His methods are those of job description and job evaluation, task analysis and performance appraisal. The course designer in training is more likely than his counterpart in education to be able to justify behavioural specification of learning outcomes, and it is not surprising to find that the works of Robert Mager are widely read and applied in the training sector. After all, the competences of interest to the trainer are frequently the behaviours themselves. It is all the more surprising, therefore, that an activity so clearly susceptible to computer 'treatment' should have figured so marginally in the spectrum of Programme applications.

It may be useful to consider briefly the types of job to which CAT might be applied. Our choices here will be illustrative rather than exhaustive.

Technician/specialist: this job category is represented in the NDPCAL by the Post Office and RAF Locking (SAFARI) applications of CAL to electronic fault-finding, and arguably by a similar diagnostic application in the Glasgow Clinical Decision-Making Project. The Post Office and RAF projects are the clearest examples of CAL as straightforward replacements for conventional experience. The ends remain exactly the same (accurate fault-finding) but instead of working with real equipment the faults are simulated and traced through interaction at the computer terminal. These applications contain an element of CML, in that feedback helps the teacher to present the student with faults of suitable complexity, as well as checking the validity of test items.

An issue to be faced here is whether the quality of the experience is significantly altered: the technicians may prefer hands-on contact with real equipment to ensure long-term retention of what is learned, and the confidence and facility that that implies; practice effects gained through CAT would ultimately be self-defeating if such practice could not be translated on the job.

Management: applications in this category can usefully be examined in terms of Morris and Burgoyne's (1973) distinction between operational management, where the activity is readily understood, and developmental management, where the manager's activity consists in shaping his own routines. An example might be the comparison between an accountant carrying out an audit according to agreed procedures, and an accountant developing new management control procedures. It is easier to envisage instructional CAT for basic operational skills, than it is to envisage conjectural CAT where pre-determined CAT methods can teach high-level skills for the resolution of undetermined managerial problems. The developmental category must be considered on the boundary between training and education. The London Business School project, for example, avoids treating managers as in need of a describable repertoire of performances, instead seeking ways of reflecting managers' conceptual frameworks to each other.

Clerical: training standards for clerical work can be tightly specified ('the reservations clerk should be able to identify the country of a given airport in 90% of the test items presented'), and such work is increasingly concerned with computers. But relevant skills are then largely specific to the industry's or employer's computer operations, and acquired through training on the job.

The cost factor in CAT

A significant factor, whatever the job category, is the very different level of student costs in the industrial training sector, and the implications this has for the power balance between provider and consumer. During management education, a middle manager might cost his company a salary of £9000, plus sizable overheads, and a further £250 per week in course fees, which produces a student cost of £10 per hour. The Post Office technicians, with wages and accommodation included, cost £206 per week of training. True, this gives greater potential savings to any successful CAT application: but it also implies greater costs if an application fails, and heavier accountability to the paying customer. A corollary is that the manager or unionised technician may feel less willing to accept the impositions of a coercive CAT experience: his student labour has to be clearly authentic. A further corollary is that the costs of low reliability are much more apparent. The Post Office project suffered poor service from an albeit temporary time-sharing computer, which left technicians kicking their heels. And the London Business School project once had 50 even more expensive managers facing a two-day hiatus when the local mini-computer crashed. Such students cannot easily be re-timetabled, or asked to come back in their free time. A further point on available technology is that both Post Office and SAFARI projects have found difficulty in replicating complex circuit diagrams on VDU terminals: Post Office technicians are expected to divide their attention between a printed manual and the VDU screen, whilst the RAF was experimenting with a second terminal to display microfiches of circuit diagrams.

Education and training

Perhaps the major issue for the future of CAT concerns the viability of the older concept of 'training'. Training, by traditional definition, limits options while education extends. It concentrates on performance rather than the kind of attention to principle that would allow the learner to generate his own code. In a society faced with the likelihood of successive 'retraining' for the changing conditions of employment it is doubtful whether training can remain for much longer within a narrow rubric of task analysis unrelated to broader 'educational' issues.

Concluding overview

Innovations cannot always be careful about the company they keep and they run the risk of being damned by association. The computer in the classroom is a newcomer, quite unfamiliar to the vast majority of teachers who will be asked, sooner or later, to consider whether it could help them do a better job. But all of them, like the rest of us, know something about the uses of the computer in other areas of their lives, from the relatively mundane calculations of payslips to the exotic selection of a mate. For many it epitomises the depersonalisation of their relationships as individuals to those who employ them, those who manage them, and those who administer the services and exact the demands that society legislates. Its ubiquitous role in organisational life is seen as symptomatic of the technologisation of society, a process popularly associated with dehumanisation and domination. The computer is, in these terms, the instrument of those in charge, and a symbol of their power and inaccessibility to the individual citizen.

This image of the computer is a response to its social history, itself critically influenced by investment costs, which ensured that commercial development would primarily exploit applications of use to organisations which could both afford the capital investment and hope to recover the costs by improving their efficiency. Large business firms and government departments were, and remain still, the principal customers for a facility which, even in its crudest technological form, delivered a quantum leap in their capacity to store, retrieve, and process information for decision making.

This dominance by prestigious customers is rightly a cause of concern, and a reason for watchfulness. The educational consumer in some sense plays second fiddle; the available technology is likely to be shaped by the requirements of others.

But, even if we concede that the computer is the instrument of those in charge, it does not follow that computer assisted learning, as it assumes a role in education, will increasingly paraphrase its role in society at large. We would contend the contrary. In Britain at least, the teacher keeps the gate of the educational process. He is, despite periodic challenges to his professional autonomy, 'in charge' of the classroom encounter. The NDPCAL strategies of teacher-led development and teacher-to-teacher diffusion constitute both an acknowledgement and an endorsement of this basic fact of curriculum power. The diversity of CAL developments within the Programme testifies to the educational pluralism which such a system of individualised power promotes, a diversity of educational values, aspirations, and practices which defines the conditions for a successful technology. That the technology of computing has the potential to meet such conditions should not be in doubt. It must be clear from our account of CAL that a technology which can already, despite a development history largely devoted to bureaucratic needs and mass marketing values, sustain a wide range of pedagogic thrusts, is essentially non-determinist in character.

This is not an argument against vigilance, and certainly not an endorsement of the apparent indifference of the educational community to the stirrings of computer assisted learning. Our purpose in this chapter is to assist that community to pursue a vital evaluation question — what educational uses of the computer ought to be encouraged?

But to engage the constructive interest of the community in this issue is no mean task, as the experience of the National Programme has made clear. Indifference is widespread, pervasive, seemingly unshakeable. It has something to do with the social symbolism of the computer, something to do with a generalised technophobia, something, perhaps, to do with a deep sense of personal impotence in the face of technology-based change — a belief in technological determinism.

The computer is widely seen as a threat (those who dispute this will look in vain for support in the rhetoric of politicians) and the persistence of this perception continues to frustrate a balanced review of CAL options. Certainly the opportunity for such a review is now with us. The National Programme has explored and defined some of the options, and has laid out its wares for inspection. The next two or three years offer a period for reflection and evaluation before the next major policy thrust in computer-based education can be initiated.

There are dangers, should the opportunity be overlooked, dangers spelled out by Raymond Williams in the context of televisual technology:

'. . . the history of broadcasting institutions shows very clearly that the institutions and social policies which get established in a formative, innovative stage — often *ad hoc* and piecemeal in a confused and seemingly marginal area — have extraordinary persistence into later periods, if only because they accumulate techniques, experience, capital or what to some seem prescriptive rights.'

Computing is the one certain technology of the future. In the education process, some of its possibilities are now accessible to public and professional judgement. The future is being shaped now.

References

AUSUBEL, D P and ROBINSON, F G (1969) *School Learning*, New York: Holt, Rinehart and Winston

AYSCOUGH, P (1977) *CALCHEM: Final Review Report,* Department of Physical Chemistry, The University of Leeds

BLOOM, B S (1970) 'Mastery learning' in Block, J H (ed), *Mastery Learning: Theory and Practice*, New York: Holt, Rinehart and Winston

BRUNER, J S (1966) *Towards a Theory of Instruction,* Cambridge, Mass: Harvard University Press

CARBONELL, J R (1970) *Mixed Initiative Man-Machine Instructional Dialogues,* Cambridge, Mass: Bolt, Beranek and Newman

COWAN, J (1976) 'Must self-instructional materials be firmly structured and directed towards lower-level objectives' in Clarke, J and Leedham, J (eds), *Aspects of Educational Technology X — Individualised Learning* London: Kogan Page

FINE, B (1962) *Teaching Machines,* London: Oak Tree Press

FREEDLE, R O and CARROLL, J B (eds), (1972) *Language Comprehension and the Acquisition of Knowledge,* New York: Holt, Rinehart and Winston

GAGNE, R M (1970) *The Conditions of Learning* (2nd ed) New York: Holt, Rinehart and Winston

GLASER, R (1968) 'Adapting the elementary school curriculum to individual performance' in *Proceedings of the 1967 Invitational Conference on Testing Problems*, Princeton: Educational Testing Service

HAWKRIDGE, D (1974) 'Problems in implementing computer managed learning' *British Journal of Educational Technology* **5**, 1

JAMISON, D, SUPPES, P and WELLS, S (1974) 'The effectiveness of alternative instructional media: a survey' *Review of Educational Research*

KEMMIS, S (1976) *The Educational Potential of Computer Assisted Learning: Qualitative Evidence about Student Learning*, University of East Anglia: Centre for Applied Research in Education

MACDONALD ROSS, M (1972) *The Problem of Representing Knowledge*, Paper to the Structural Learning Conference, Philadelphia

MAGER, R F (1962) *Preparing Objectives for Programmed Instruction,* Palo Alto, California: Fearon

MORRIS, J and BURGOYNE, J G (1973) *Developing the Resourceful Manager,* London: IPM

PAPERT, S (1970) 'Teaching children thinking' *Proceedings of the IFIP Conference on Computer Education*, Amsterdam. (Reprinted in *Mathematics Thinking*, Bulletin of the Association of Teachers of Mathematics, No 58, 1972)

PIAGET, J (1971) *Psychology and Epistemology*, trans Arnold Rosin, New York: Viking Press

POPPER, K R (1974) *Conjectures and Refutations: The Growth of Scientific Knowledge* (5th ed), London: Routledge and Kegan Paul

ROCKHART, J F and SCOTT MORTON, M S (1975) *Computers and the Learning Process in Higher Education.* A report prepared for the Carnegie Commission on Higher Education, New York: McGraw-Hill

SKINNER, B F (1953) *Science and Human Behaviour*, New York: Free Press

WILLIAMS, R (1974) *Television: Technology and Cultural Form*, London: Fontana Paperbacks

For further details on the UNCAL evaluation write to Barry MacDonald, Centre for Applied Research in Education, University of East Anglia, University Village, Norwich NR4 7TJ.

4. The costs of CAL

This chapter is written by John Fielden of Peat, Marwick, Mitchell & Co, Management Consultants.

'What would life be without arithmetic, but a scene of horrors'
(Revd Sidney Smith)

Background

Since the financial evaluation was commissioned in May 1973 the financial climate and prospects for education have altered radically. The notion that an independent agency should closely study the cost of projects seemed almost out of date four-and-a-half years ago. Today, as education is gradually reconciling itself to the concept of greater accountability and financial controls, the appointment of a financial evaluation has, in retrospect, an inevitable and unremarkable air.

The task of measuring the financial implications of small scale educational innovations was a novel one. Most of the relevant experience internationally was devoted to large national projects for radio or television innovations in education and used the language of the economist (UNESCO, 1977).

The problems of costing computer based innovations have been outlined at length elsewhere (Fielden and Pearson, 1978), but should be summarised briefly. The questions to be faced include:

— How should cost answers be given when enquirers have so many different viewpoints and perceptions of cost?
— How can the relative ignorance of educational audiences about costing techniques and definitions be overcome?
— What units should be chosen for measuring the impact of innovations? Is it realistic to show all charges in the common measure of money?
— Does the rampant inflation of recent years and the changing balance of cost between computer hardware and software invalidate the use of money in any one year's values?
— What account should be taken of time? Should the conventional economic techniques of discounted net cash flows or of charging interest

on the capital employed be used for the evaluation?
— How can the many assumptions and ingredients in the cost calculations be presented simply?
— Is there any point in identifying the detailed resource implications of change when the 'outcome', the quality of education provided, is probably very different in form from the outcome of conventional instruction?
— In the last resort how can the financial and the educational evaluations come together with any coherent or matching conclusions?

It would be foolish to pretend that all these problems have been overcome; some are fundamental to all educational innovation. The financial evaluation however developed a costing methodology which goes some way to meeting some of the technical problems and which could have an application outside CAL in the evaluation of other educational changes.

The methodology selected
The question 'what does CAL cost' is deceptively simple, but it has many different answers according to the perspective of the enquirer. Thus, it was essential for the evaluation to consider the requirements of the various groups of people who would ask this question. Analysis showed that these could be grouped into three categories, each having different perceptions of cost and different expectations as to the answer. The three levels of enquirer can be defined as departmental or school, institutional (for example a university or local authority), national.

— The *departmental* enquirer in, say, a university or polytechnic, whose financial horizon is usually bounded by the institution's mechanisms for departmental budgets and who sees no link between staff time and cost. In the maintained sector, a school is the analogous level to the department. Answers to cost questions asked by such a person should therefore encompass only those expenses which fall within the departmental or school budget. As institutions vary in their attitudes to virement and to charging out the cost of central academic services, such as the computer, there is no standard answer to departmental enquirers. Any answers involving the time of staff should be presented in time units of days or weeks rather than hundreds of pounds. This emphasis on units also allows the information to be used in relation to future prices which will be inflated above the current levels.

— The *institutional* enquirer has a perspective of his university's or local authority's accounts and the budgetary pigeonholes it contains. Like the head of a department he is conventionally only interested in extra or marginal costs (although there are signs that this attitude is changing). Unless he maintains central records on staff contact time and teaching methods he will not be interested in information on CAL development time invested by academic staff. The answer to the question 'what does CAL cost' should therefore cover the marginal impact on the central computer centre and central overheads as well as teaching departments. No concern is shown for the annual cost of capital which is omitted from university and polytechnic accounts, nor is the time factor considered.

— At the *national* level the cost of CAL enters the sphere of accountancy and economic evaluation. If the total impact on the nation is being considered, it is valid to measure factors such as the life of the material being developed, the cost of capital and the extent and phasing of development time. It is also necessary to contemplate the measurement of benefits such as teaching time replaced or laboratory equipment made redundant. If all these factors are to be aggregated, it becomes essential to convert them into the common measure of cash arriving at a total annual cost of the innovation. In both the previous cases (departmental and institutional) this approach is possible but is not required by the audience concerned and indeed will make the answers unintelligible to them.

In response to some of the other methodological problems the evaluation has been pragmatic. Different units were chosen to show the resource impact at all levels:

— for almost all the interactive CAL projects funded by NDPCAL the total cost per student terminal hour was used (defined as one student sitting at a terminal for one hour so that if two students shared the terminal two student terminal hours would be recorded)

— CML projects in secondary education and military training had the annual cost per pupil or trainee as their measure

— two projects in CAL were more realistically judged by calculating the cost per enquiry or cost per access to the computer

— in the transferability projects it was sensible to identify the cost per package or program transferred.

The evaluation tried using broadly the same methodology to measure conventional teaching costs as a comparison, where appropriate, for the unit costs of CAL and CML that it calculated. Two papers (Pearson, 1976 and Pearson, 1977) gave the teaching cost per student hour in universities and secondary schools. In addition project evaluations ascertained relevant costs such as the local authorities' capitation allowance (to contrast with the extra annual cost per pupil of a CML project) or the cost of educating one medical student (compared with the extra cost of a CAL project in medical education).

Four other aspects of the methodology deserve mention.

— Particular note was taken of the time taken to develop computer based packages. At the request of the financial evaluation almost all projects maintained records of the development time spent both by NDPCAL staff and by academic members of the institution. The request for this data discipline caused considerable lively discussion in projects. Although one cannot say that the data finally provided is an accurate indication of what happened or of what might happen in another institution where individuals possess different skills, it is nevertheless a guide. This data was used to build up a development cost for each project comprised of funding from NDPCAL and the 'matched funding' or institutional contribution to the development. The development cost represented the initial high effort of producing material which is much greater in any one year than normally would be funded internally by an institution. The development cost was then written off over an assumed life of the material.

— Capital expenditure was treated in the commercial sense with depreciation charges calculated on each category of cost according to the expected useful life. Mini-computers and terminals were assumed to have lives of seven and five years respectively.

— No account was taken of the incidence of expenditure over time by using discounting methods to show the present value. There were two reasons for this:

(i) little of the NDP's resources went on capital expenditure and most of the project costs were on staff time for which discounting techniques were of questionable relevance

(ii) no measurable cash benefits accrued from the projects and the flow of other 'hidden' benefits was hard to identify and could not be quantified with any reliability.

—Where total costs were calculated for projects they reflected the cost in the 1977/78 academic year when a 'hypothetical steady state' was assumed. It would have been unrealistic to produce a costing during the period of NDPCAL funding because there was an abnormally high level of development effort and low figures for student terminal hours. These forward looks in some cases assumed that development continued at a steady-state annual level (of about 20-25% of the course material).

Computer assisted learning in higher education

By far the largest class of projects funded by the National Programme was that covering CAL in higher education, and several of them have now reached a 'steady state' in that their initial development is complete. Because of this, it is possible to make a number of generalisations and the rest of the chapter will be devoted to this. Other sectors of education, industrial training and CML, will however be included in the final report of the financial evaluation (Fielden and Pearson, 1978), as will the military projects which were commissioned relatively late in the lifetime of the Programme and from which no firm conclusions can yet be drawn.

(*a*) *The marginal cost to a department of taking on CAL is usually low.* Since higher educational institutions have few mechanisms for charging out centrally borne costs to departmental budgets in 'real money', the extra cost of CAL is not high. For example, departments could usually expect to pay only for the maintenance of terminals, stationery and handouts, while the computer costs are financed from other budgetary pockets. Staff time on development is the main cost to departments, but that carries no budgetary implications.

The majority of the polytechnics involved in NDPCAL gave their projects access to the central computing service, which do not charge departments for the use of computer time or terminals. There is thus no financial entrance fee to the CAL Club. (Most of NDPCAL's university projects on the other hand used either a central dedicated CAL mini-computer or a departmental machine). Since more than 200 CAL packages are now available for transfer to higher educational institutions, it will be possible for individual academic staff to import these and, if they can find suitable terminals, to provide CAL for their students. This small scale application has been termed 'experimental' or 'planned use' by the NDPCAL in its Future Study Report *CAL in Higher Education — the Next Ten Years* (NDPCAL, 1977). There are unlikely to be any major financial barriers to such small-scale work given the two prerequisites of academic time and computer/terminal availability.

(*b*) *CAL will always be an extra cost overall*. CAL has many applications in the teaching curriculum — as an illustrative aid in large lectures, a mathematical and calculation tool in examples classes or tutorials, a substitute or a supplement for laboratory experiments, an occasional replacement for small tutorials and in one project the central core for a whole new course. Most of these applications of CAL in both tutorial and laboratory mode are an addition to students' contact time. In only some projects does a session at the terminal replace timetabled staff contact and then staff usually make the freed time available for tutorial and remedial guidance. Where replacement occurs, it is certain that, taking other applications of CAL in the institution and the past development costs into account, there is no overall saving. CAL is thus usually a classic example of the cost-effectiveness dilemma: a claimed qualitative improvement for a clear extra cost.

It must be emphasised that CAL as a major innovation in teaching practice would inevitably be an addition to curricula while it was still untried and novel. There are already, after four years, several instances of courses being revised to include CAL formally in the timetable. This process will become more common as CAL is accepted. In the CUSC project, for example, replacement is the general rule and only a few packages are an extra for the students.

Some projects find that a package which one institution uses as an extra tutorial aid (or for revision purposes) is taken as a substitution for laboratory experiments or examples classes by another institution (both the CALCHEM project and Leeds statistics project reported this).

(*c*) *Budgetary structures in higher education can mask the real costs of CAL*. The use of the three-level approach in costing usually produces the following results:

— CAL brings benefits to a department at very little marginal cost
— CAL can cost an institution up to £20,000 a year extra, see (*f*)
— the cost of CAL at the national level shows it to be more expensive per student hour than other innovative teaching methods.

Since much of the decision-making concerning the adoption of CAL will be taken at departmental level where all the benefits and few of the costs are to be found, it is therefore possible for decisions to proceed with implementing and using CAL programs which do not take all the resource implications into account. This point implies that budgetary and decision-making structures in higher education need to be adjusted so as to identify the moment when potentially expensive innovations are under consideration.

(*d*) *Only in very few cases will CAL provide more than 20 hours formal contact per student per annum.* Since CAL is usually an extra in the curriculum at this point in its development in the UK, there must be a limit to the extent to which staff will increase both the curriculum content of students and their own contact time. In addition the development of CAL packages is very labour intensive, unless they are imported through a program exchange, and demands a heavy personal commitment from those engaged in it. There are also likely to be professional academic reasons for limiting the involvement of CAL, since some staff will feel that they may be losing vital feedback on individual student performance and some may also still distrust a medium with which they are not wholly familiar. Another reason for the limit to CAL exposure is a practical one of timetabling and cost. Even where a university CAL service exists, a department is unlikely to be able to obtain access to more than 20 terminals at a time. For many class sizes this will mean booking more than one session. Most timetables in science subjects are relatively inflexible and have few gaps. The harder it is to fit in extra sessions at terminals the greater becomes the risk of uncoordinated timing, as lectures and tutorials fall out of sequence with the CAL packages at the terminal (which are intended to support them). Thus, as a general rule one hour per student per week at a terminal seems to be an achievable norm. Taking into account the build-up of theory at the beginning of most courses and the fall-off of formal contact at examination time, 20-30 hours a year is thus likely to become the normal practical exposure to timetabled CAL for any one student. There are places where these levels are exceeded (University of Exeter's School of Engineering Science and the Physics Department, University of Surrey), but this is because students are encouraged to use the terminals for self-programmed problems and individual tasks as well as formal CAL packages.

(*e*) *The time taken to develop CAL packages varies considerably but many science packages have absorbed between 200 and 400 hours of effort in their development.* Although the key factors are clearly the scale of the package and the complexity of the subject matter, statistics on package development time show that it is rare for science packages to require less than 100 hours of development effort. The packages concerned vary in length of use from 20 minutes to 3 hours. Records have been kept in some projects of the three categories of development effort; technical effort related to the computer program, educational effort on the content of the package and supporting educational effort on any handouts, worksheets or notes associated with merging the package into the course. This analysis identified packages where the development effort was disproportionate to the possible use. If, for example, a package could only help the 40 students on one course for one hour, someone should ask whether it was worth 400 hours of development effort. In CALCHEM the Director of the project has suggested that a package which has involved, say, 300 hours of development effort should be used for at least 300 student hours in total.

There is a difference of opinion between projects on whether or not a learning curve can be relied upon to reduce package development times. No one denies that experience makes programmers and academic staff more adept, but some suggest that the production line benefits do not materialise because staff prefer to move on to produce more challenging packages so that no time reductions are achieved.

(*f*) *Two typical structures for CAL in an institution have different incidences of cost.* While it is possible to embark on CAL in a very small way, any growth in demand will soon affect institutional budgets. Two typical ways this demand can be met are shown opposite in Figure 8.The central university services would usually be linked organisationally to the Central Computer Service and the departmental mini could be one of many independent machines.

In addition there could be other variable costs related to usage, such as Post Office charges, extra tapes and computer stationery and the printing costs of handouts and educational material for CAL sessions.

If the central CAL service is adopted, departments will receive the benefits and the costs will be borne centrally from the institutional budget. If a dedicated mini-computer is acquired, most of the £9700 costs shown are likely to be charged to the faculty or departmental budgets.

(*g*) *It is unusual to achieve terminal utilisation figures in excess of 500 hours per terminal per annum.* Since graphic display terminals cost at least £3500 it is important to maximise terminal utilisation. Early estimates of a reasonable maximum use have proved too optimistic, eg 750

	Central CAL service	Departmental or faculty mini-computer
	£	£
Capital costs of computer	60,000	20,000
Capital costs of terminals		
Graphics display	17,500	7,000
Teletype / VDU	20,000	10,000
	97,500	37,000
Extra operating costs		
Computer maintenance	6,000	2,000
Terminal maintenance	2,600	1,200
Programming staff	12,000	6,000
Other direct costs, insurance etc	750	500
	21,350	9,700

Figure 8. Typical costs of CAL in higher education institutions

hours per terminal per annum; and the evaluation has concluded that too many factors (such as the academic programme, the '9 to 5' mentality, the cost of janitorial attendance after 5 o'clock, the laboratory's demands on the timetable, and the peaking of lectures and tutorials in morning sessions) act as constraints when one attempts to expand terminal use. Some single subject projects in the National Programme were unable to use their terminals for more than 250 hours per annum. These were in subject areas closely linked to laboratory sessions, where UGC norms for laboratory utilisation (16 hours per place per week) are rarely achieved in some universities. There have been two NDPCAL projects where terminal use has exceeded 500 hours per annum (equivalent to just under 20 hours per week during a 26-teaching-week year).

(*h*) *Total cost from the national point of view for CAL shows a figure of £15,000 - £30,000 pa for most institutions.* National generalisations about CAL mostly relate to its total cost, that is the cost to the nation calculated according to the conventions adopted by the financial evaluation agency. This cost includes the following elements:

— development cost: one year's share of the accumulated development cost during the period of NDPCAL funding
— capital costs: depreciation charges on the capital equipment
— annual operating costs including staffing, maintenance, etc
— share of institutional overheads related to the project.

In arriving at these costs many assumptions have had to be made. Some of these assumptions are sensitive and have affected the final costs calculation significantly. Because of this the total cost figures are not precise or definitive and should be regarded as indicative only. However, the same methodology was applied to all the projects' costings, so that the resulting figures can at least show costs relative to each other.

It must of course be remembered that the educational aims and content of projects differ greatly so that the costs should not be looked at in isolation. Packages also vary substantially in their complexity and size; some tackle complex concepts and absorb 2-3 hours of a student's time, while others will be in the instructional or calculation mode and will take less than half an hour to work through or use. Because of the large number of special factors influencing the costs of each project, the cost per student terminal hour of each project has not been shown. In Figure 9 opposite the expected total cost and student usage for the 1977/78 academic year is given for some of the major NDPCAL projects. All those listed have achieved a 'steady state' in the sense that the bulk of their development is over and the annual running costs assume only a minimal level of future (internally funded) development.

The student hours shown relate only to the logged terminal use in the institutions named. In several cases the packages developed were transferred to other institutions (outside formal National Programme arrangements) and are being used with students. Statistics on this use are not available. A rigorous application of the costing methodology would take this use into account and would charge the receiving institutions an element of the initial development costs. This would have the effect of lowering the costs per student terminal hour in the parent institution. Some projects (eg, Engineering Sciences Project with 74 transfer 'events') were particularly energetic in arranging such transfers and their costs are therefore overstated.

A further complication in the derivation of unit costs is provided by the problem of projects which use packages for demonstration purposes in lectures with large TV screens. In the CUSC project 525 students met packages in this way in 1976/77. The difficulties of costing this in any

Project/Institution	Total cost per annum	Student terminal hours
Leeds Statistics Project		
Leeds University	34,520	5,500
Leeds Polytechnic	10,700	1,400
Engineering Sciences Project		
Queen Mary College	42,800	2,100
Exeter University	28,300	4,400
Computational Physics Teaching Laboratory		
University of Surrey	29,000	5,500
Clinical Decision Making Project		
University of Glasgow	33,700	4,400
CALCHEM Project		
University of Leeds	11,730	820
Open University	6,620	1,750
Basic Mathematics Project		
University of Glasgow	20,580	3,275
CUSC Project		
University of Surrey	32,800	1,200
Chelsea College	28,500	350

Figure 9. Total costs and student terminal hours, 1977-78

realistic manner are so great that all use of this kind has been ignored in the data in Figure 9.

In view of the unfamiliar cost elements introduced into the total costing a further presentation of the project cost data might be helpful. Figure 10 therefore shows for each of the above-named institutions the extra cash cost of the project in 1977/78 from the point of view of the institutional budget, together with the percentage of the total cost represented by past development expenditure.

In calculating the marginal cost some subjective judgements have had to be made. The question has been faced by considering what cash the institution would actually save if the CAL activities were closed down. Thus, where a dedicated computer exists its maintenance and insurance costs would immediately be saved, but where a shared central service is used, the service is assumed to continue despite the cessation of CAL on it.

A comparison of the statistics in Figures 9 and 10 shows the substantial difference between marginal ('institutional') and total ('national') cost in all projects. Much of this is accounted for by the large amount of resources invested in the development of the packages and programs.

(*i*) *The total national cost per student terminal hour of CAL in higher education is unlikely to be less than £4 and will usually be in the range of £5 to £10.* One project exists where the cost is less than £4 and several are at a state of development where low student terminal hours produce costs well in excess of £10.

Project/Institution	Marginal cost to institution £	Development expenditure as percentage of total cost %
Leeds Statistics Project		
Leeds University	6,040	34
Leeds Polytechnic	2,350	30
Engineering Sciences Project		
Queen Mary College	14,900	28
Exeter University	3,900	12
Computational Physics Teaching Laboratory		
University of Surrey	13,700	38
Clinical Decision Making Project		
University of Glasgow	13,500	36
CALCHEM Project		
University of Leeds	620	54
Open University	2,070	30
Basic Mathematics Project		
University of Glasgow	3,600	60
CUSC Project		
University of Surrey	14,800	32
Chelsea College	9,800	45

Figure 10. Marginal costs and development expenditure, 1977-78

(*j*) *The marginal cost of university teaching by more conventional means falls in the range of 60p to £2.50 per student hour depending on the subject and group size.* The evaluation has calculated the marginal cost of a conventional university teaching session (Pearson, 1976; Pearson, 1977) as a point of reference for the CAL costings. The methodology has had to take a top-down/macro perspective as opposed to the detailed micro perspective used for the CAL exercises; as a result there are different problems and inconsistencies in the two approaches. We would therefore not wish the comparison to be relied upon or quoted without qualification. The two most important qualifications are as follows.

— In looking at the costs of CAL side by side with those of conventional teaching we are not necessarily comparing like with like. In particular, CAL is a very individual form of learning commonly used for those parts of a course where the concepts are particularly difficult; CAL often enables students to get a feel for the problem to an extent which might take much longer by conventional means. The costs of conventional teaching on the other hand refer, at the lower end of the range, to a lecture with an average class-size of 25 or, at the upper end of the range, to a tutorial for six students or a practical laboratory session.

— The costs of conventional teaching include only academic staff time and their direct support staff. Also, they are marginal costs intended to reflect the average extra cost in the long term which would be incurred by an institution if an extra hour's teaching were provided on a permanent basis. Therefore they take no account of accommodation, materials or institutional overheads and, while they include an allowance for lecture preparation, this is intended to cover the routine situation and makes no allowance for the initial development of a department's curriculum. They are thus more comparable with the marginal costs given above for CAL than with the total costs.

(*k*) *The number of special factors influencing the cost of CAL make generalisations difficult.* After the expenditure of so many resources on CAL it ought now to be possible to identify the features of a project which are expensive and those which reduce cost. Unfortunately this ideal is not achievable in any precise way. There are so many variable factors influencing each project (personalities, skills, institutional finances to name only three) that no generalisations are possible. At best therefore we can only summarise some of the features which in some projects cause a low cost per student terminal hour. These are as follows:

— 'popularity' of the topic concerned, and durability against changing interpretations or academic fashions
— flexibility of the packages to allow shared use by two or more students working unsupervised at the terminal
— geographical proximity to enough terminals to permit use by a whole class at a suitable time in the teaching syllabus
— commitment to CAL as a teaching method by enough senior staff in the subject concerned so that terminal contact becomes a formal part of the course rather than an informal voluntary part
— the import of packages developed elsewhere with no major modifications other than related printed course material
— development by experienced staff after full planning of the academic content and the objectives of the package in the course
— emphasis on documentation of programs and other techniques to ease the transfer of packages elsewhere
— enthusiasm and drive of the initial academic entrepreneurs which can gain support and eventually additional users for existing CAL systems.

The key factor is without doubt student numbers. Projects which produce packages in esoteric subject areas taken by only a few students for part of a course will obviously be very expensive. On the other hand service teaching offers a fruitful area for large numbers and lower unit costs.

(*l*) *There will be few or no cash savings from CAL.* American literature on CAL in higher education contains several claims for savings which, it can firmly be stated, are unlikely to be achieved in the United Kingdom. (The claims are not actually realised in the USA either!) Military training may achieve savings through CAL, since in the USA several of the current applications are claiming to be cost effective (Miles, 1977). The principal area of potential economies in higher education would be the saving of equipment by the use of simulation packages (as in the RAF with flight simulators). In practice, however, very few CAL applications in the National Programme replace laboratory experiments, as the emphasis is more on undertaking experiments that could not be carried out in any other way or on highlighting conceptual issues in support of laboratory work. At Queen Mary College, however, the terminals have been used to carry out an experiment which would otherwise have required a piece of equipment costing £6000. Also in the CUSC project it was suggested that there may be small savings because of less demand for laboratory consumables and that in the long term some equipment might not need to be replaced. Such minor realisable economies are all that one might expect to set against the cost of embarking on CAL.

(*m*) *Very considerable savings of development time have occurred because of the NDPCAL's encouragement of inter-institutional projects and the stress on transfers of CAL material to other staff outside the formal projects.* Projects have kept good records on outside recipients of their packages and in the case of the Engineering Sciences, CUSC and CALCHEM projects these have often included overseas institutions. Unfortunately it never proved possible to obtain information on the use made of packages by the importing institutions, as the real measure of effective transfer. On the other hand evidence of the economies resulting from common development of packages abounds in project records, and several evaluation meetings heard of packages which were absorbed into another institution's computer system within hours rather than weeks.

Conclusion

The nation has spent about £5 million on CAL and CML in the projects under the NDPCAL (£2.6 million direct funding plus an estimate of matched funding). By the standards of British educational innovation this is a very large sum. by American CAI and CAL standards it is not so large. In only a few projects can the total cost per student terminal hour approach that of conventional teaching in a laboratory or a small-group tutorial. In military training however there are indications that the American experiences of cost-effective applications of CAL and CML could be repeated. Unfortunately the British military projects began too late in the life of the National Programme for final conclusions yet to be possible. There is little doubt that in most CAL educational projects the total cost is much higher than for conventional instruction and that none of the early claims for realisable savings of staff time or cash can be supported.

Against these relatively harsh cost verdicts must be set some very important qualifications. CAL is often very innovative educationally and is frequently teaching a subject that could not be taught in any other way. Conventional topics are also taught, some projects claim, in a way that enhances students' understanding which would not otherwise be possible except by intensive tutorial sessions. These and other qualitative claims have been considered in Chapter 3.

Thus, the point must be made that there should surely be some advances in teaching technique which are 'worthwhile' despite their extra cost. CAL and CML are however extremely high cost technologies and are the most expensive tools yet introduced into the teaching process, however one costs them. There is no doubt that some of the NDPCAL's projects, which are at the top end of the cost spectrum and which have few claims to major educational change, are likely to be considered not cost-effective. Similarly some projects with lower unit costs and claims for a changed or improved educational content should satisfy educational decision-makers who are faced with the real value judgement about cost-effectiveness.

It is not the function of the financial evaluation to answer these issues, but merely to summarise the key resource implications and to highlight the levels and interpretations of cost. In doing so it may have set some new guidelines for assessing the impact of educational innovations; it will certainly have made the exercise more complex and subjective than many believed possible. If this can help to remove the unquestioning and often naive acceptance of cost figures in educational decision-making the evaluation will have achieved something.

References

FIELDEN, J and PEARSON, P K (1978) *The Cost of Learning with Computers: Report of the Financial Evaluation*, London: CET

MILES, R J (1977) *Computers in Military Training in the 1980s. A Future Study Report,* Technical Report No 18, London: National Development Programme in Computer Assisted Learning

NDPCAL (1977) *CAL in Higher Education — the Next Ten Years. A Future Study Report,* Technical Report No 14, London: National Development Programme in Computer Assisted Learning

PEARSON, P K (1976) *The Cost of Conventional Teaching in Universities,* Technical Report No 13, London: National Development Programme in Computer Assisted Learning

PEARSON, P K (1977) *Costs of Education in the United Kingdom,* London: Council for Educational Technology

UNESCO(1977) *The Economics of New Educational Media*, Paris: UNESCO

PART THREE

HOW THE PROGRAMME WORKED

Part Three looks at the way in which the Programme went about its task, the strategies developed, the procedures and methodologies adopted. The ideas in Part Three whilst being rooted in a particular innovation concerning the computer, may be of interest to people and funding agencies involved in other research and development work in education and training. In the closing chapter of Part Three, the Director assesses the strategies adopted and how well they were implemented.

5. Terminology

'. . . care taken to choose and use more accurate terminology pays dividends in the attitudes of teachers and the public towards new developments' (Holznagel, 1977, p 32).

One of the first tasks that the Director undertook in the first days of the Programme was to try and clarify terminology. The research literature is thick with acronyms and differing definitions. Many of the conflicting views about computer assisted learning find their source in problems of definition.

The task of defining terms continued throughout the Programme's life, with a range of people contributing to the debate. Definitions changed over time, in the attempt to make them more rigorous and realistic. For example, computer managed learning (CML) was defined in the beginning as a subset of computer assisted learning (CAL). Later on, it seemed sensible to accord CML separate but equal status with CAL, given the differing characteristics of the two applications.

The easiest way into a definition of CAL and CML is to say what they are not. Fairly obviously first of all, they are not research applications of the computer. Most of the university computing in the UK is used for research purposes. Secondly, and less obviously, CML is to be differentiated from administrative applications of the computer, for student records, teachers' pay, library automation. Thirdly, and least obviously, CAL applications are to be distinguished from computers being used as the object of instruction. CAL (teaching *with* computers) has very different educational objectives to computer education (teaching *about* computers). The boundary lines between CAL/CML and research/administrative/computer education applications are not clear-cut.

Computer managed learning

Computer managed learning (CML) presents fewer problems of definition than CAL. In the research literature, CML (and its American counterpart CMI — computer managed instruction) tends to have a fairly consistent meaning. CML applications involve the computer in helping the teacher to manage, rather than provide, learning opportunities. Four functions of the computer can be identified. First, the computer can mark, generate, and analyse tests, either for diagnostic or examination purposes. Secondly, the computer 'routes' the student, on the basis of previous test results, stored profile characteristics of that particular student, or expressed options, through an individualised course. The individualised course can be 'taught' in a number of ways — conventional teaching, self-instructional modules, experimental and project work. Thirdly, the computer stores and updates classroom records. Fourthly, the computer reports on progress to the individual student, the teacher, the course developer, the administrator or training manager.

The heart of a CML application is the routing function. In general, an application which involves test-marking but not routing would not normally be defined as computer managed learning.

CML applications overlap with those administrative applications which concern student records and timetabling/scheduling. In the United States CML applications are merging with administrative data processing, to achieve cost-effectiveness through shared use of common data bases (Holznagel, 1977). Certain computer software techniques, to do with data management systems, are likely to accelerate this trend (bringing with them problems of 'privacy').

Computer assisted learning

Computer assisted learning (CAL) was defined eclectically within the Programme, to encompass two rather different 'traditions' of teaching with computers. The first, and most familiar, tradition derives from the programmed learning movement of the late 1950s. Here, the computer provides 'individualised instruction', that is to say teaching adapted to the requirements of the individual learner. The significant feature of the second tradition, dating from about 1964 at places like Dartmouth College, New Hampshire, is

'that references to individualisation, to educational psychology and technology, are seldom if ever made. Instead the language of justification is the language of the particular subject matter for which the computer is employed. The uses of the computer, here, derive not from learning theory or even educational considerations, but *specifically from the requirements and nature of the subject matter* (Hooper, 1974, p 363).

Computer as tutor

In the first tradition, normally called CAI (computer assisted instruction) in North America, the computer acts as a kind of machine tutor, teaching facts or skills on an individual basis, or as a kind of 'exerciser', giving the individual graded drill and practice in facts or skills already introduced in some other way. An example of the tutorial approach, from a chemistry program developed by the CALCHEM project, is shown in Figure 11. This type of teaching, done at a teletype terminal, is obviously reminiscent of programmed learning but is much more like a tutorial conversation. For example, the student is able to make free constructed responses to the computer which is programmed to 'understand' them and respond accordingly, whereas in programmed learning the student tends to be restricted to multiple choice-type questions.

```
IN THIS SECTION, YOU WILL BE ASKED TO DECIDE WHICH QUANTITIES YOU
ARE GOING TO MEASURE IN ORDER TO FIND E*.
FIRST READ PAGE 1 OF B9Ø1L IN THE VISICARD, THEN TYPE Z.

Z ←

CAN YOU MEASURE E* DIRECTLY?  (ANSWER YES OR NO)

NO ← CORRECT

TO FIND E*, YOU LOOK AT RELATIONSHIPS INVOLVING E* WITH
  A) OTHER QUANTITIES WHICH CAN BE MEASURED, OR
  B) OTHER QUANTITIES WHICH THEMSELVES CAN BE RELATED TO MEASURABLE
     QUANTITIES
DO YOU KNOW OF ANY RELATIONSHIPS INVOLVING E*?  IF SO NAME THEM.

THE ARHENIUS EQUATION ← YES

WE HAVE SEEN THAT E* CAN BE FOUND USING THE ARRHENIUS EQUATION.
WHAT DO YOU ACTUALLY MEASURE?

RATE CONSTANT AND TEMPERTURE ←

YES, WELL DONE.  YOU NEED TO MEASURE THE RATES OF THE REACTION AT
DIFFERENT TEMPERATURES, BUT WHAT DO YOU ACTUALLY MEASURE TO FIND
THE RATE?

CONCENTRATION ←

YES, MEASURE THE CHANGE IN CONCENTRATION WITH....(COMPLETE)

TIME ← GOOD

THERE ARE THREE THINGS TO MEASURE.  IE. THE CHANGE IN CONCENTRATION
WITH TIME AND THE TEMPERATURE AT WHICH THE REACTION IS OCCURRING.
```

Figure 11. Extract from CALCHEM program

The tutorial/exerciser type of computer assisted learning is defined by the existence within the computer software of two main models. First of all, there has to be a model of the teaching (or routing) function, for example embodied in an instruction to the computer such as: '*If* the input by the student at this point is greater than 80 or less than 15, *then* the computer will respond as follows "Rubbish, think again!" ' Secondly, the software for tutorial applications must contain a model of the learner, for example with the computer 'knowing' that a particular pupil is weak in a given subject area.

Computer as laboratory

The second tradition of computer assisted learning sees the computer acting as a learning resource, rather than as a teaching medium. The phrase 'computer as laboratory' has been coined within the Programme to describe the range of applications of the computer as a tool for calculation, simulation and modelling, problem-solving, data base manipulation and retrieval. The most familiar example of the computer as laboratory in industrial and military training would be the digital computer-based simulator, as illustrated in Figure 12. An educational example is shown in Figure 13, where the student is using the computer via a graphics terminal to explore a physical system modelled within the computer. In neither case, is the computer involved in direct teaching. That is done by live teachers and instructors (or supplementary written materials) alongside the computer system. The CAL application takes on a tutorial flavour at that moment when a part of the teaching function performed by the live teacher is *recorded* into the computer software itself.

David Tawney of UNCAL has written a detailed essay on the terminology of 'computer as laboratory' and on those very slippery terms 'simulation' and 'modelling'.

'Modelling is the process of *creation*, *adaptation* or *choice* of a theoretical model to correspond with a natural phenomenon or a man-made system. In CAL it leads to a software model embodied in a computer, that is, to a *simulation*. Inseparable from modelling is the testing of the model for fit, using the simulation. Underlying it is the particular status of the model: its adequacy is under suspicion. A *simulation* is a system constructed to embody a theoretical model in a way which allows the parameters of the model to be varied and the effects readily observed .... In a simulation the status of the model is different; it is *not* under suspicion' (Tawney, 1976, p 13).

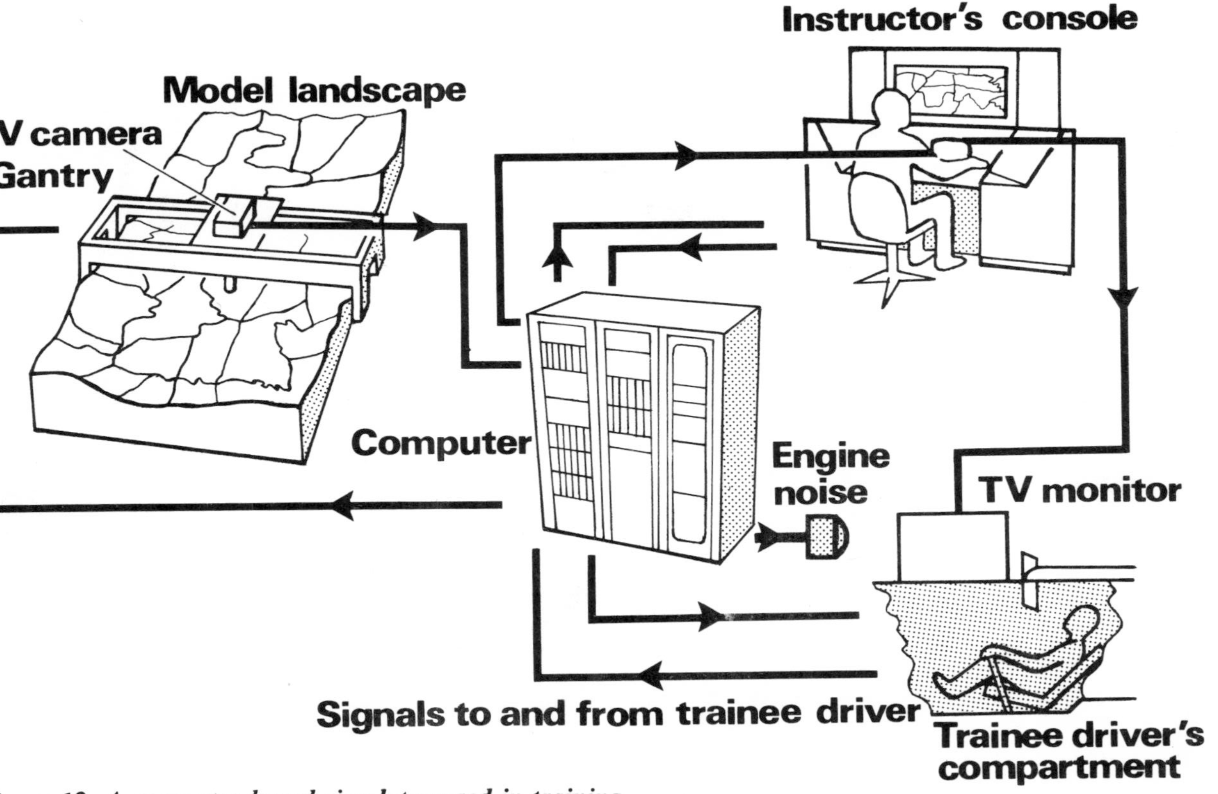

Figure 12. A computer-based simulator used in training

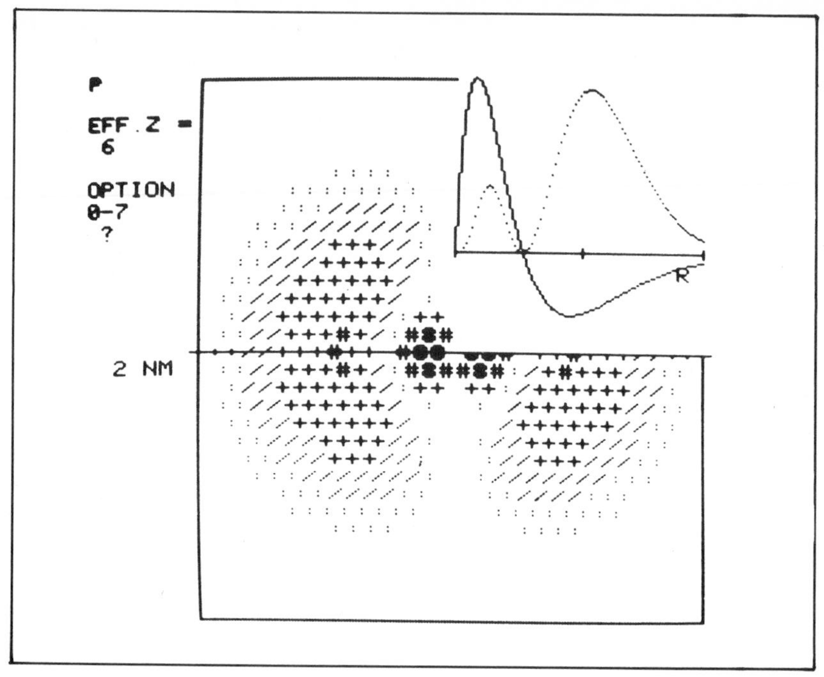

Figure 13. Graphics screen display from a CAL package on atomic orbitals (CUSC)

One of the political strengths of 'computer as laboratory' applications, by contrast to 'computer as tutor' applications, is that they tend always to be very close to, if not actually overlapping with, research applications of the computer. As a result, the 'computer as laboratory' concept has less difficulty being accepted as academically respectable.

Finally, computer as laboratory applications can be categorised by mode of computer use. The student either interacts with the computer using prewritten programs, without needing to know how to use a programming language, or, the student writes his own programs for the computer. Most NDPCAL funding was devoted to projects, which developed prewritten programs for use by students in 'laboratory' mode.

Tutor/laboratory hybrids

A feature of recent CAL developments, within and outside NDPCAL, has been the growth of teaching programs which combine tutorial and laboratory traditions, and which combine prewritten programs with opportunities to program the computer directly. The CAL work, based at Leeds University, is an example. In these hybrid teaching programs the essential feature is the provision of facilities for modelling and simulation within a tutorial framework. Two kinds of adaptivity are present. The presentation of the subject matter adapts to the individual student's progress, for example in the type of feedback provided. In addition, the subject matter itself, for example, a mathematical model of a chemical system, adapts according to the way in which the student manipulates parameters and values.

CAL/CML hybrids

The distinction between CAL and CML systems outlined is not always easy to make in practice.

'One criterion that has been used to distinguish CML systems from those using the computer as a tutor or laboratory is whether instructional materials are actually held and administered by the machine. CML systems manage but do not administer. However any CAI [tutorial] system which stores information about the student from one lesson to the next is impinging on CML territory while trends in CML systems towards turning assessment tests into learning situations are moving CML towards a tutor role' (Rushby, 1977, p 2).

The title CAMOL (Computer Assisted Management Of Learning) acknowledges this merging of CAL and CML roles. Under the CAMOL system, students receive along with the results of computer-marked tests short bursts of remedial teaching, linked to routing instructions, as illustrated in Figure 14. A similar approach, which has been in regular use at the RAF Staff College (FS 3/22/01) for three years, has proved to be very acceptable to students.

CML and tutorial (but not laboratory) CAL systems overlap in a crucial area. Both contain in the computer programs a model of the individual learner which is progressively built up, and a routing function (the particular route through 'frames' of teaching stored in or outside the computer selected according to given student responses). Conceptually this is the most difficult area for CAL and CML development. It is also the area which causes resistance amongst teachers, who see the routing function as a central element of live teaching, as something that often cannot be predetermined and therefore cannot be automated. To guard

```
    CAMOL SYSTEM   REPORT: RE1   RESULTS SLIP   VIA  C/O SCIENCE EDUCATION, PHASE 1     DATE: 24/03/77    PAGE 1

207              HARRY MCMAHON

COURSE: DE380        INFORMAL TEST FOR: ST2    TEST: 202

                                                            YOU SEEM TO HAVE MOST OF THE PRE-REQUISITES TO MODULE 1:
                                                            INTERPRETING GRAPHS/FREQ.TABLES, USING BASIC TERMINOLOGY.
                                                            READ COMMENTS & FOLLOW SUGGESTIONS FOR ANY SINGLE ITEMS
                                                            MISSED IN PARTS 1&3.  YOU SEEM TO HAVE A SLIGHT PROBLEM WITH
                                                            DIFFERENTIATING OBS,INF,HYP & OP,DEF.  READ THE COMMENTS FOR
                                                            ITEMS MISSED & FOLLOW THE SUGGESTIONS.  IF YOU NEED HELP/
                                                            OTHER RESOURCES, SEE YOUR TUTOR.

RESULTS              SCORE/MAX.

     FULL TEST          34/  37        . . . . . . . . . . . . .  DIAGNOSTIC TEST B

     PART-SCORE 1       13/  14        . . . . . . . . . . . . .  GRAPHS & FREQUENCY TABLES (Q.1-14)

                2       10/  13        . . . . . . . . . . . . .  DISTINGUISH BETWEEN STATEMENTS OF OBS,INF,HYP&OP DEF(Q15-27)

                3       10/  10        . . . . . . . . . . . . .  "DEF. & CONCEPTS" CHAPTER 1 CHASE (Q.28-37)

     QSTS TO BE ANSWERED  37

  Q.NO     SCORE  CONF  ANSWERS

0/015       1.00           A   CORRECT

0/016       1.00           B   CORRECT

0/017       1.00           C   CORRECT

0/018       0.00           B   NO; THOUGH IT MAY BE WORDED LIKE AN INFERENCE, THERE IS
                               NOTHING TO BACK IT UP.  IT DOES TELL HOW AN IDEA CAN BE
                               DEFINED IN MEASURABLE TERMS, AN OPERATIONAL DEFINITION.

0/019       1.00           B   CORRECT

0/020       0.00           D   NO; THIS SAYS NOTHING ABOUT RELATIONS BETWEEN CONSTRUCTS AND
                               HOW WE MIGHT ESTABLISH AN OBSERVABLE DEFINITION, IT IS AN
                               HYPOTHESIS.
```

Figure 14. Student printout of the CAMOL system showing test results and routing comments

against these problems, CML systems usually have an override facility, which allows teacher or student to reject machine routing decisions.

Conclusion

Using the definitions set out here, the National Programme's 35 projects and feasibility studies (listed on pp 18, 19) can be categorised as follows. The largest proportion by far — 15 — have developed laboratory CAL applications. Only one project (Glasgow mathematics, DP 1/10) took a purely tutorial CAL approach, whereas four (Leeds statistics and CALCHEM, DP 1/01B and DP 1/06A, and RAF Locking and the Post Office, FS 3/03A and FS 4/03) combined tutorial and laboratory roles. (The Post Office project also used a CML feature of the IBM/ITS software, to manage fault-finding exercises on the real equipment after the tutorial/laboratory session at the computer terminal. The CML feature proved particularly attractive to instructors.) Nine projects developed CML work, with CAMOL and the RAF Staff College combining some CAL functions with CML, as noted above. Four projects were active in administrative applications (timetabling, scheduling and information retrieval). One project, Culham Laboratory's machine translation service (TP 22/03), is not classifiable in these terms since it was concerned purely with technical problems of transferability.

This leaves one project, Computer Assisted Learning in Upper School Geography (FS 2/03) at Birmingham University, which does not despite its title really fit the classification system. Here, the computer's role was to store and produce teaching materials in modern geography which could be used in the classroom *without* access to a computer. Another example of the computer as 'producer' would be films made by using computer-generated animation (Francis, 1975).

The definitions of CAL and CML developed within the National Programme are not entirely satisfactory. The definition of CAL, for example, does not really accommodate the use of the computer as a possible means of teaching *about* the computer — for example, the use of CAL to teach programming languages to computer science students. The problem here is distinguishing between the use of the computer as *object*, and as *medium*, of instruction. Only the latter can be labelled CAL. Another difficulty with the CAL definition is that it is probably too broad. CAL comes to mean, taking the logic of the NDPCAL definition to its extreme, *any* use of the computer in teaching or learning. So, for example, a student using the computer to calculate a standard deviation is doing CAL.

By the end of the Programme, there were some signs that these labels — CAL, CML — were anyway beginning to outlive their usefulness. In the United States, increasingly the term 'educational computing' is being used to refer to the wide range of applications of teaching with and about the computer, without any great concern for precise definitions.

References

FRANCIS, A M (1975) 'Computer produced audio-visual materials' in Hooper, R and Toye, I (eds) (1975) *Computer Assisted Learning in the United Kingdom — Some Case Studies,* pp 103-118, London: Council for Educational Technology

HOLZNAGEL, D C (1977) 'A comparison of computer managed learning in the USA and UK' in Rushby, N J (ed) (1977) *Computer Managed Learning in the 1980s. A Future Study Report* (pp 31-45), Technical Report No 16, London: National Development Programme in Computer Assisted Learning

HOOPER, R (1974) 'Making claims for computers', *International Journal of Mathematical Education in Science and Technology*, **5**, 4, pp 359-368

RUSHBY, N J (ed) (1977) *Computer Managed Learning in the 1980s. A Future Study Report*, Technical Report No 16, London: National Development Programme in Computer Assisted Learning

TAWNEY, D A (1976) *Simulation and Modelling in Science Computer Assisted Learning,* Technical Report No 11, London: National Development Programme in Computer Assisted Learning

6. The management of development

This chapter describes the approach that evolved during the Programme to the management of development funding. By comparison with other funding agencies in education, the approach had a number of novel aspects.

The Programme began life at a time of widespread concern about the management of research and development. People were beginning to question the centralised models of funding curriculum innovation adopted by the Schools Council in England and Wales, and similar agencies in the United States. Yet, traditional academic research funding in higher education was seen to have drawbacks caused by inadequate central control — parochialism, duplication, unsystematic coverage of the research domain, lack of evaluation, poor project management.

The National Programme's approach to funding can best be described under five main headings.

1. The role of the central Programme Directorate in 'cooperative' funding
2. Programme and project management
3. Strategies to promote institutionalisation
4. Strategies to promote transferability
5. Evaluation procedures (see next chapter)

1. The role of the central Programme Directorate in 'cooperative' funding
The Directorate of the National Programme, based in London, was small. In the middle years of the Programme, it contained five executive and three secretarial/administrative staff. The working patterns adopted by the Directorate differed quite markedly from those of central staff in research councils. For example, the Directorate was given more independence than is normal for research council staff. The executive Programme Committee empowered the Director to refuse applications for funds without necessarily referring the matter to Committee. The Directorate was encouraged by officials at the Department of Education and Science to formulate a coordinated policy within which all funded projects were embedded, rather than behave in the more *ad hoc* manner of grant-giving agencies.

The biggest difference, however, following naturally from this delegation of power, was to be found in the style of working. Whereas traditionally research council staff are responsive, reacting to applications for funding as they arrive, the National Programme Directorate was assertive. (In recent years, there has been a move in research councils towards more assertiveness, for example, the Social Science Research Council's Research Initiatives Board).

The assertive style of working in the Directorate is best illustrated by examining how projects came to be funded. For a start, there were no standard application forms sent out. Ideas for projects originated in different ways. Some arrived conventionally through the post in the form of letters requesting funding for a particular application. Other ideas for projects developed within the Directorate in London, and would then be suggested to particular people — who, in some cases, had not thought of applying for funds, and in one case did not even know there was a National Programme!

In whatever way the ideas may have originated, the actual design of projects became a collaborative affair, involving prolonged negotiation (in one schools project, as long as a year). This period of negotiation allowed the Directorate to get to know and evaluate potential project staff (and *vice versa*). It allowed the Directorate to feed into the design of the project certain 'national' requirements, for example, that any teaching materials to be developed with NDPCAL funds should be made as transferable as possible. Similarly, the future project staff were able to feed in their 'local' requirements; for example, to do with local political problems of support (one project director asked to be exempt initially from independent evaluation because of adverse reactions to the idea amongst key academic staff).

On a few occasions, negotiations broke down because one or other side could not agree to certain conditions, and no proposals emerged. More usually, a mutually acceptable proposal did emerge, which was usually written by project staff and edited by the Directorate. These proposals were then placed for approval before the Programme Committee by the Director or Assistant Director, who in 1976 and 1977 each managed a group of projects; but they did not always bear much resemblance to the first ideas. This is one of the reasons why the Programme did not have standard application forms (though the proposals to Programme Committee did follow a standard format). Another reason was the feeling that good proposal writers do not always make good project directors, and *vice versa*.

Both during the period of project design and negotiation, and after the project began to be funded, the active style of working required members of the Directorate to travel extensively (in 1974, Assistant Director Roger Miles covered 15,378 miles within the UK). Behind a written application for funds, or a written annual report, are people, institutions, political climates, which are best evaluated at first hand.

2. Programme and project management

From the beginning, attention was paid to the need for good Programme and project management. This emphasis caused tension between the Directorate and some of the university-based projects in the early days of the Programme.

There were a number of reasons for emphasising the importance of management. If, for example, an innovation does not 'take', it is difficult to know which variable — the management or the innovation itself — is mostly to blame. Also, within the computing industry at large, project management has been a growing concern. The success of large computer projects is likely to depend as much on management, as on technical, proficiency.

Another reason was the time-scale of the Programme — five years. If objectives were to be reached within the short space of four academic/school years, then productivity needed to be high from the start. Also, the inter-institutional nature of many of the projects required resolute direction if they were not to collapse under the weight of committees and poor communication.

Finally, and probably most important of all, this emphasis on management within the National Programme came out of the early 1970s' anxiety about research and development. At the time when the National Programme was starting up, some of the experimental medical computing projects funded by the Department of Health and Social Security were getting into severe difficulties caused by bad budgeting, cost and time overruns, inadequate control, communication and evaluation procedures (Her Majesty's Stationery Office, 1976).

In the first two years of the Programme, John Fielden, in addition to his work as financial evaluator, assisted both the Programme Directorate and projects in setting up viable management systems (NDPCAL, 1975). He recommended, for example, the use of four-monthly accounting periods which enabled the Directorate and projects to keep a regular watch over actual spending compared to estimated spending. Project proposals contained detailed estimates of costs over the life of the project, divided into four-monthly accounting periods.

Another budgetary technique was 'virement'. Project directors were permitted, within certain limits, to move (vire) money allocated under one heading (for example, staffing) to another heading (for example, non-recurrent expenditure) in the light of changing circumstances. It was in the interest of projects to husband their resources since any money saved would probably not be lost to the project.

An important role in project and Programme control was played by 'stepped' funding, via the mechanism of midterm evaluation. The midterm evaluations, carried out by the Directorate at the end of each step of project funding as a prelude to any further step of funding, enabled project directors and the Programme Directorate jointly to revise objectives, plans, and resource requirements, on a regular basis. Development projects, by their nature, change as they grow and learn.

3. Strategies to promote institutionalisation

The reasons for choosing institutionalisation as the main aim of the Programme were given at the beginning of Chapter 1. A group of strategies evolved over the years with the express purpose of accelerating the chances of institutionalisation. The strategies were multidimensional because institutionalisation of innovation was viewed by the Programme as a political process involving many factors. In the USA, the lack of good, cost-effective software is seen as the major obstacle to CAL's acceptability. This is, in the Programme's experience, at best a half-truth.

Seven strategies to promote institutionalisation were used:

(a) The choice of location of projects
(b) Organisational structure and the choice of project director
(c) Matched funding
(d) Critical mass
(e) Curriculum integration
(f) 'Riding the educational wave'
(g) Recommending the closure of the Programme.

(a) The choice of location of projects

The first strategic decision in pursuit of institutionalisation concerned the choice of location of projects. For CAL and CML to survive, projects had to be based close to the sources of power. This meant two things. First, given that power in the British educational system is distributed widely, projects had to be spread across more than a few select universities. Secondly, within any given institution, the project should be located close to the sources of institutional power. In the higher education projects, this meant that projects were located not in the educational technology or educational research departments, which are on the periphery of institutional power, but in the mainstream teaching departments — physics, chemistry, mathematics. The director of the Computational Physics Teaching Laboratory project at the University of Surrey (DP 1/03A) was the Head of the Physics Department.

At schools level, for the same reasons, projects (with one exception) were located directly in local education authorities and not in universities which has been the Schools Council tradition. It should be noted that local education authorities proved, in the Programme's experience, to be as capable of managing large development projects as universities.

In military training, by contrast to education, power is far more centralised — within the Ministry of Defence in London. As a result, NDPCAL's military projects, whilst being geographically located in Catterick Camp or RAF Locking, were designed, evaluated and managed in close cooperation with MOD personnel at the centre.

(*b*) *Organisational structure*

Following on from the location of projects, there were particular concerns about organisational structure in projects and about the choice of project director. Who reports to whom, who is on which committee, are highly relevant to the success and failure of institutionalisation.

The choice of project director was particularly important because development — the prelude to institutionalisation — is personality-dependent. Does the project director have academic credibility? Can he or she manage? Can he or she present results in a convincing way? Does the director know the way around the corridors of power locally? Finally, can the director make himself over time *dispensable* (by delegating and spreading power and responsibility) since too much personality dependence will make for fragile institutionalisation? Such assessments were, not surprisingly, difficult to make, and, given their personal and subjective nature, a cause for anxiety.

(*c*) *Matched funding*

'Matched funding' was a specific strategy used to strengthen the chances of future institutionalisation. Unlike many research funding agencies, the National Programme did not as a general rule pay overheads. Project institutions were required to contribute resources alongside NDPCAL funding. These resources were usually staff time, accommodation, and computing facilities — some of it measurable in terms of real cash to the institution, some of it being 'below the line' costs.

The existence of the matched funding requirement encouraged the involvement of decision-makers at the project's inception, thus preparing the ground well in advance for the vital institutionalisation decisions later on. In the Hertfordshire schools computer managed project, for example, officials from County Hall were involved, through matched funding, at the project negotiation stage. Indeed one of them came with the project director to a meeting of a sub-committee of the Programme Committee in the autumn of 1973 to discuss future funding. The same official, four years later, was to play a key role in the (successful) negotiations for post-1977 institutionalisation. Another function of matched funding is that it softens the financial transition to local budgets at the end of external funding, since parts of the project are already paid for locally, are already 'in the estimates'.

(*d*) *Critical mass*

The strategy of 'critical mass' was premised on the belief that an innovation which is in *widespread* use across an institution or local authority or country will acquire the broad base of support and visibility that is difficult to stop. At the national level, it led to the funding of a small number of large projects, rather than a large number of small projects. At the local level, projects set out to develop computer applications that would involve increasing numbers of teachers and learners. In January 1977, in an institutionalisation negotiation in one of the higher education projects, the project director pointed out to the university that if the CAL work were not continued, 3000 hours of student teaching from October 1977 would need to be provided from somewhere else.

(*e*) *Curriculum integration*

The strategy of curriculum integration tries to ensure that CAL and CML developments happen within a framework of broader curriculum and course redesign. This is to avoid the innovation remaining (it usually has to start life as one) an optional extra, which can be discarded in times of trouble. At Imperial College, for example, within the Engineering Sciences Project, a group of third-year courses in heat transfer and fluid flow were totally redesigned around a computing core. If CAL were to be discarded, then the courses themselves would have to go.

(f) 'Riding the educational wave'
The Programme attempted to develop those innovations that reinforced existing trends within education and training systems. For example, CAL and CML applications were favoured which complemented moves towards resource-based and individualised learning.

(g) Recommending the closure of the Programme
The closure of the Programme at the end of five years ensured that projects concentrated their attention on institutionalisation, and is the only real way of permitting the aim of institutionalisation to be objectively evaluated.

4. Strategies to promote transferability
The reason for choosing transferability as a twin aim of the Programme was set out at the beginning of Chapter 2. Transferability was seen primarily as a human and attitudinal problem, rather than, as is the tendency in North America, a technical problem to do with computing technology. Also, the Programme came to question the conventional wisdom that the problem with transferability (or dissemination as it is more usually called) is just a 'communication problem', and that dissemination failure can be attributed solely to failures of communication.

'The "problem of communication" is a product of the rhetoric of curriculum development rather than of the reality. The rhetoric is premised on an unexamined assumption: that all of us concerned with the education of pupils — teachers, administrators, advisers, researchers, theorists — basically share the same educational values and have overlapping visions of curriculum excellence. A confirmation of the argument is the proposition that if there are major discrepancies between the advocacies of the support groups and the behaviour of the practitioner groups . . . then there is *prima facie* a problem of communication . . . All this is not to say that there are no problems of transmission which can be accounted for in terms of poor presentation: of course there are. But curriculum innovators face a much more significant problem which needs to be distinguished from this but is often confused with it: the issue of whether people want to hear what they have to say. The answer does not necessarily lie in saying it more clearly' (MacDonald and Walker, 1976, p 44).

The Programme evolved six main strategies for transferability.

(a) Inter-institutional projects
(b) Personal contact
(c) Existing communication channels
(d) Program exchange centres
(e) Presentational skill
(f) Technical policy (see Chapter 8)

(*a*) *Inter-institutional projects*

The keystone strategy for promoting transferability was the funding of inter-institutional projects. Inter-institutional funding was a departure from the tradition of 'centres of excellence' which was implicit in the NCET recommendations of 1969, and in the way in which closed-circuit television was introduced into British universities after 1967. In inter-institutional projects, dissemination is seen as part of development, not as an afterthought. Throughout the design of teaching material, decisions of an educational and technical nature can take into account the differing requirements of a spectrum of potential users, thus making the end product easier to disseminate. There is of course always the danger that the teaching material will become such a compromise of different interests that no one will actually use it. Inter-institutional projects multiply the number of participating teachers and therefore the likelihood of future institutionalisation via critical mass. Inter-institutional projects, designed as cooperative federal networks, grow organically as interest grows. They are based on the belief that teachers (and administrators) will more readily adopt an innovation if they have participated in its development. This reduces the power of the NIH (not invented here) syndrome. It also enables the conflicting, non-consensual values of the participants to be voiced early on, thus reducing the so-called 'communications problem'.

Different types of inter-institutional project evolved. The CALCHEM project based all its production in two centres (Leeds University and Sheffield City Polytechnic), with the nine collaborating institutions agreeing in advance what was to be produced centrally for which institution(s). By contrast the Engineering Sciences Project distributed production of CAL packages amongst all six cooperating institutions, with a central coordinating office at Queen Mary College, London. The CUSC project spread production amongst the three leading institutions (UCL,

Chelsea and Surrey) but with each institution taking primary responsibility for one of the three chosen science disciplines.

(b) Personal contact

House, in his aptly titled book *The politics of educational innovation*, wrote: 'To control the flow of personal contact is to control innovation. As the flow of blood is essential to human life, so direct personal contact is essential to the propagation of innovation .... Who knows whom and who talks to whom are powerful indicators of where and when an innovation is accepted, or if it is accepted at all' (House, 1974, p 6). Personal contact was a central strategy for promoting transfer of ideas, experience, and teaching materials. NDPCAL made a special point of allocating money to enable project staff to travel. Inter-project visits, intra-project meetings, meetings with prospective adopters, conferences and workshops, overseas travel, were all encouraged. 'We are, after all, trying to address ourselves to practising teachers who are not particularly interested in educational research as such . . . the project has expanded very satisfactorily without the support of weighty analysis and impressive publications. Our conclusion is that *those who have pursued their investigations of CAL to the point at which they have a reasonable grasp of what we are doing, recognise that the real evidence they seek can only be obtained by observing the system in action* . . . dissemination of this particular innovation has occurred almost entirely on a person-to-person basis and by direct observation' (Ayscough, 1976, p 6).

(c) Existing communication channels

Personal contact was strengthened by exploiting the existing communications channels used by practising teachers, for example the Chemical Society or the Geographical Association. NDPCAL worked with these professional associations, setting up workshops, journal articles and special publications. In initial encounters with CAL, chemistry teachers, for example, will listen to other chemists, and not to educational technologists or computing specialists.

(d) Program exchange centres

As part of its transferability strategy, NDPCAL funded some program exchange schemes. Activities of these centres included the maintenance of a catalogue, operation of a program library, 'standards setting', teacher training, consultancy, 'salesmanship', the encouragement of new software development. In line with the ideas set out in (c) above, the geography package exchange (GAPE, TP 22/06A) was funded to operate under the auspices of the Geographical Association.

(*e*) *Presentational skill*

Presentational skill was emphasized early on in the Programme as an important, yet often overlooked, component of transferability. Audiences have differing requirements for information, and differing attitudes to mode of presentation. Choice of language is all-important. Computing and educational technology language may put off the customer, whereas a few scrawled equations may attract him.

(*f*) *Technical policy*

Finally, whilst NDPCAL favoured a view of transferability which emphasised human factors, technical considerations could not be overlooked. The Programme's policy on technical transferability is set out in Chapter 8.

Conclusion

The Programme's approach to funding consciously included elements of what might best be described as an 'obstacle course' arrangement. To establish the worthwhileness of an innovation involving the computer, when relatively generous external funding is present, methods are needed to test the resilience of the innovation and the innovator. At the project design and selection stage, NDPCAL drove fairly tough negotiations to flush out the fortune-hunters from the committed practitioners. The addition of the inter-institutional component, and the requirement for institutionalisation, meant that the particular innovation had to win acceptability from a wider range of people beyond the pioneer enthusiast.

Finally, it should not be inferred from this chapter that the Programme was the sole inventor and proprietor of the various strategies outlined. Many of the ideas were imported from other organisations such as the Open University, the Schools Council and the Nuffield Foundation. The concept of 'matched' and 'stepped' funding derived from North American experience, for example. The overall strategy was the product of many people within and outside the Programme and much transferability.

References

AYSCOUGH, P (1976) 'Academic reactions to educational innovation', *Studies in Higher Education* **1**, 1

HER MAJESTY'S STATIONERY OFFICE (1976) *Sixth Report for the Committee of Public Accounts,* Session 1975-6, London: HMSO

HOUSE, E (1974) *The Politics of Educational Innovation*, Berkeley, California: McCutchan Publishing Corporation

MACDONALD, B and WALKER, R (1976) *Changing the Curriculum,* London: Open Books

NDPCAL (1975) *Control and Reporting Systems for Development Projects*, revised edition, London: National Development Programme in Computer Assisted Learning

7. Evaluation procedures

This chapter is written by Roger Miles, Assistant Director, NDPCAL.

Even in 1973 money was tight and it was obvious that many critics were poised to pounce on the slightest hint of profligacy. There was no escaping the facts: computers were expensive and £2 million was a large sum to expend on one educational technology programme. Hence it was crucial that the Programme made every effort to foster demonstrably worthwhile activities and prepare a sound base for its defences on the subject of costs. Educational and financial evaluation were necessary to shape the work and provide summative evidence at the end; they were to be important tools of management at every level of authority within the Programme.

During the life of the Programme the issue of accountability in education became much more prominent and, together with the worsening financial situation, placed even greater weight on evaluation. In fact, evaluation was so widespread that some people wondered if the Programme suffered from over-evaluation. Certainly the evaluation raised issues not always considered by educational planners and financiers, and all the Programme's affairs were scrutinised closely.

Ironically the evaluation itself — rather than CAL — sometimes appeared to be among the most controversial aspects of the Programme. Tensions between proponents of different evaluation methods and resistance from sceptics — for example, those doubtful of the feasibility of the financial evaluation methods — generated much debate. The Directorate allowed considerable diversity to flourish and at times encouraged it, feeling that it was an inevitable result of the wide range of interests and experience contained within the Programme. The volatile and in some parts uncertain nature of the evaluation art was also clear and a further reason for promoting experiment with novel methods.

The Programme's approach to evaluation

The Programme's approach to evaluation was novel in both the style adopted and, by many standards, the large proportion of resources devoted to it. The reasoning behind the emphasis on *responsive* and *formative* evaluation was primarily the need for a capacity to make necessary mid-course corrections quickly and effectively. However, the overall desire was for an *illuminative* evaluation that would inform participants, and assist decision-makers, as well as telling the story of the whole experience, warts and all.

The sharp distinction made between research and development when setting the Programme's aim had a profound effect on every aspect of the activity including the evaluation. It highlighted the need for an evaluation that would run in parallel with the development, be responsive to problems as they arose, and keep decision-makers well informed throughout. Unlike a formal research design which controls events to test specified hypotheses, the evaluation was not to constrain development but rather to proceed eclectically picking up information likely to contribute to improvement and understanding of the innovation being attempted.

Empiricism is deeply rooted in the conventional wisdom of evaluation and is the natural choice for those faced with the problem of assessing the merit of an innovation. This is particularly true in educational technology where the dominating methodological influence is experimental psychology, itself firmly based on positivist empiricism and concentrated on mechanistic models of man. This approach seeks to describe and explain human behaviour in terms of man being passively subject to external influences. It uses controlled experiments to unravel the causal connections between those influences and behavioural outcomes, very much as the physical scientist manipulates processes in the laboratory.

The pressure on educational innovators to adopt this methodology is great, despite the widely recognised difficulties of formulating hypotheses amenable to testing in this fashion, developing adequate measurement techniques, and running the trial with sufficient control of all the variables. Since educational technology has made extensive use of these methods, many expected the National Programme to follow suit and base its evaluation on controlled comparisons of CAL and conventional teaching methods.

However, the Directorate was very conscious of the limited success of past research of this type for probing practical issues in education. Also, as Wrigley (1976) described, an alternative style of evaluation had grown up in the last decade for monitoring major curriculum development activities. Thus a prominent development agency, the Schools Council, saw the evaluator as part of the project team acting as a 'critical friend' rather than a detached researcher. Wrigley presents this new-style evaluator's role as: 'helping the developers define their objectives, producing measuring instruments when necessary, but also using various rough and ready procedures to measure the outcomes of the work'.

As one would expect in any novel area of activity there is considerable variation among evaluation practitioners as how best to proceed and what the crucial issues are. New-style evaluators disagree, for example, on how far they should go in drawing conclusions and making recommendations as opposed to concentrating on presenting a portrayal of the issues and leaving decision-makers to form their own conclusions. Some draw their methods predominantly from psychology; others favour sociological or anthropological perspectives. There is, therefore, a good deal of disagreement and debate among evaluators and the whole area appears not a little confused.

Nevertheless the main thrust of this new approach was reasonably clear in 1973 and it seemed to offer an evaluation better suited to the aims and circumstances of the Programme than traditional experimental methods. Thus it was envisaged that evaluation would use a wide range of methods to study the CAL innovation closely in context and collect information useful for management and in developing explanatory concepts.

Such thinking was not entirely new to educational technology. Holland (1961) discussed the futility of applying experimental methods to the often asked question: 'Are teaching machines more effective than conventional methods?' The central problem Holland identified was that neither variable is specified in any general sense and so differences attained will only relate to that particular situation. Instead, Holland argued, each potential user of programmed learning materials should examine them carefully and then evaluate them by closely observed trials in the classroom on which judgements, not comparisons, can be made.

In an important paper on social research methodology Cronbach (1975) argued that the experimental research model of gradual progress towards generalisations and lawful relations, through systematic and successive experimentation, is inadequate for a study of social situations in which there are many complex interactions and things are constantly changing. He argued for closer study of the details of situations and events and that the urgency to make generalisations should be postponed in favour of constructing a complete picture of the particular. A number of other writers have contributed related arguments to support the emergence of a new rationale for social inquiry. For example, Harré and Secord (1972) proposed an alternative concept of the nature of science to that derived from positivist philosophy which has so strongly influenced experimental psychology and in turn educational technology. They call for a science of social behaviour based on a view of man as an active agent whose purposive behaviour may be explained in terms of his intentions and reasons rather than external causes. Such a science would emphasise not laboratory experiments and quantitative measurement but rather focus on investigation of single cases and examination of exchanges between people through observation and interview. It would also emphasise the need for empirical data gathering to be informed and guided by theoretical analysis and conceptual development.

This new philosophical view of the nature of social science, particularly social psychology, has great significance for the new-style educational evaluator who sees the introduction of an educational innovation as a complex social event rather than a problem reducible to a form amenable to experimental treatment. It adds considerably to the strength of the philosophical and theoretical base which many of these evaluators are striving to create for their activities.

The National Programme's educational evaluation is the largest new-style evaluation attempted in this country. It must therefore offer an important case study for those concerned to improve the techniques and theoretical underpinning of evaluation practice. Results of the Programme's investment in evaluation may also be of interest to decision-makers and funding agencies considering the possibility of adopting such methods. The remainder of this chapter will describe the often overlapping evaluation responsibilities of the Programme Directorate, the independent evaluators, the projects themselves, and the Programme Committee.

The Directorate's evaluation activity

The Programme Directorate acted as purchaser, user and promoter of evaluation. As principal officer of the Programme, the Director was responsible for negotiating contracts with the independent educational and financial evaluators, facilitating their access to all aspects of the Programme, and coordinating the presentation of their reports to Programme Committee. He had no right of veto on these reports but on one occasion did refer a report back to its author for reconsideration; certain facts were disputed and the criticism of project personalities was considered unnecessarily severe.

The Directorate's main concern with evaluation was to obtain generalisable information on educational, technical and organisational issues and to assist managerial control. The Directorate developed two formal evaluation procedures; the midterm evaluation visit and the final review meeting.

Midterm evaluations

The midterm evaluation comprised a two-day formal visit to the project by a team consisting of the Director and Assistant Directors, the Programme Committee's nominee on the project's steering committee and two invited external assessors chosen for their expertise in the subject of the project and their independence from the Programme. After Mrs Frewin, Assistant Director (Technology), left the Programme, a third external expert was invited to cover the computing aspects. The independent educational and financial evaluators were also present, contributing both to the discussions and the subsequent reporting to Programme Committee.

These visits consisted of three sessions spread over two days and began with a presentation and examination of the project's work to date. Plans for the future, including funding required, were then considered in the second session. The final session was a 'closed' meeting of the evaluation team and independent evaluators at which views and judgements were exchanged. Responsibility for recommending continuation of the project was retained by the Director. The purpose of this final session was to transmit information and opinions rather than arrive at a verdict. A high degree of consensus characterised most of these sessions.

Following the visit the Director prepared a draft report which was circulated to the external assessors for comment. The assessors had the right to submit dissenting opinions direct to Programme Committee but none in fact did so. The Programme Committee then received the Director's report, together with reports on the project's claims and progress from the independent educational and financial evaluators, and in most cases a proposal for continued funding.

In the period December 1974 to December 1976, 20 midterm evaluation visits were undertaken. The formality of these occasions reflected the Directorate's belief that a project team's organisational skill is revealed in formal presentations, as well as their clarity of purpose and strength of argument. Experience supported that opinion; projects which presented their case well at midterm proved with one exception successful in NDPCAL terms. On the other hand, those projects which only just managed to clear the midterm hurdle continued to find the going difficult.

Only two projects were terminated at the end of step one and their difficulties had been apparent before the evaluation visit. Overall, there were many surprises and several evaluations resulted in project plans being drastically revised before further funding could be recommended.

The visits were demanding for all concerned but frequently most enjoyable. Often project staff had put a great deal into preparing documentation, display material and presentations; some complained that the disruption of their work was out of proportion with the funds being sought. Certainly the pressure on some individual project directors or managers was rather excessive and an 'anticlimax' reaction was a common cause of further loss of productivity afterwards. Where a project's shortcomings were revealed, often through sharp exchanges, the normally good relations with the Directorate suffered considerable temporary damage. A few projects failed to appreciate what was involved, were ill-prepared to give a good account of themselves and suffered in consequence.

The midterm evaluation visits were very much a formative evaluation device. A different procedure was needed in the final year for summative evaluation. Accordingly final review meetings were planned as one-day visits to each project to gather information at first hand and form a judgement of the project's achievements and failures.

Final reviews

Twenty-five final reviews took place from November 1976 to November 1977. The visiting team consisted of the Director, Assistant Director and Information Officer of the Programme, the Programme Committee nominee and the independent evaluators. No external assessors were used but several project directors invited local administrators and others likely to influence the project's prospects of survival beyond December 1977.

The shape of the first of the meeting's three sessions was determined by six pre-circulated questions from the Directorate. Question one called for data for academic years 1975/6 and 1976/7 on the numbers of students using CAL, total terminal hours or contact hours, numbers of academic staff involved in developing and using CAL materials, the number of participating institutions and a record of transfer events. Question two asked for a summary of all materials produced, tested and publicly available. The third requirement was a summary of total project expenditure. The fourth question asked projects to advance any claims for the value of CAL, supported by evidence. Question five asked, 'If you had your time over again, what would you do differently?' The final request was for a report on progress towards institutionalisation.

The second and third sessions of the final review were educational and financial critiques of the project chaired by the independent educational and financial evaluators respectively. Sometimes projects amended this timetable to focus on particular points.

Compared with the midterm evaluations these final reviews were generally much more relaxed, with projects confident in the knowledge of their achievements. The required information was obtained, though with some difficulty in cases where the project had not produced the numbers in the format requested. There were a few echoes of the resistance to costing details that was a feature of earlier negotiations with projects. As with the midterm evaluations there were a number of surprising outcomes. Tensions increased markedly in a few cases when unexpectedly disappointing results or previously unrecognised problems were revealed.

The final reviews gave the Directorate and the independent evaluators an opportunity to sharpen generalisations about the Programme as well as conclusions about each project.

The independent evaluators

The background and factors leading up to the decision to fund the two independent evaluations are well documented in the earlier report, *Two Years On* (Hooper, 1975). The two selected were the independent financial evaluation by John Fielden of Peat, Marwick, Mitchell & Co, Management Consultants, and the independent educational evaluation led by Barry MacDonald of the Centre for Applied Research in Education at the University of East Anglia. It should be emphasised that both began work in the summer of 1973, just as the first projects were being set up and when both could influence the choice of evaluation aims and methods.

In Part Two of this report are chapters by the directors of each evaluation presenting their conclusions on CAL and CML (as distinct from their evaluation of the National Programme). Both have also reported widely on their methodology (Fielden, 1974; MacDonald, 1977). A brief description of their approach to evaluation follows. For a fuller treatment of the financial evaluation methodology, see Chapter 4.

Financial evaluation

Until this study began, the costs of CAL had received only brief consideration in the United Kingdom. Ambitious claims of great potential savings by CAL developers went largely unchallenged. The problem facing John Fielden was to find a practical method of identifying and taking account of all the resource implications of creating and using a CAL system.

The process began with assisting the Director to establish a project control and reporting system which would aid identification of costs and resource implications as well as being a management tool.

Project directors were encouraged to record time spent on the project by themselves, funded staff and other colleagues, under various headings which separated development work from operational use. They were also asked to keep running totals of hours of use of CAL materials, record any changes in courses resulting from CAL use and to identify facilities and resources used.

The problem of inflation was overcome by identifying costs in terms of basic units, for example man hours, rather than money. This would allow future users of the data to apply current values to the resources needed. An important part of the methodological innovation was to identify costs at three levels:

1. the impact on the teaching department (or school)
2. the cost to the institution (or local authority)
3. the total national cost.

An important innovation was the creation of a single index of the operational cost of each project in a steady state. This unit is the cost per student terminal hour and much fun was had at evaluation meetings with projects and evaluators disagreeing over the elements to be included in this calculation. Fielden and Pearson were quick to warn of the qualitative and subjective elements in financial evaluation and urge caution in using quoted figures.

UNCAL

The UNCAL team undertook a 'new-style' evaluation, to use the distinction made earlier. The novelty of their approach created some confusion and led to difficulties in relating to others who viewed evaluation differently.

UNCAL adopted the following definition of evaluation: 'Evaluation is the process of conceiving, obtaining and communicating information for the guidance of educational decision-making with regard to a specified programme'.

The main features of their aims were:

1. to encourage self-criticism within the Programme by providing an 'outsider's view'
2. to advise projects on their own evaluation methods
3. to help the Directorate by giving independent checks on their observations, additional evidence and alternative views
4. to assist the Programme Committee by providing studies of projects and reports on general issues
5. to disseminate the ideas and work of the Programme so that the interested community at large can profit from the experience.

The UNCAL team were concerned to develop and present in-depth portrayals of each project's aspirations and achievements, and the issues surrounding the work. They sought to represent assessments by others rather than make explicit judgements themselves, and to make evaluation a democratic process by negotiating the release of reports with the people studied. The men from UNCAL went out of their way to avoid becoming 'Centre spies' for either the Programme Directorate or Programme Committee. Another feature of UNCAL was a concern for the community at large as an audience for reports on the Programme, as well as the Programme Committee and various professional groups. In their interim report, published in 1975 and called *The Programme at Two*, the team stated: 'If UNCAL fulfils its aims, its reports will provide the basis for corroboration and challenge of claims made from within the Programme' (MacDonald *et al*, 1975).

Project evaluations

A feature of the Programme's overall evaluation effort was the projects' own in-house evaluations. The Director's aim that projects should be led by subject-matter experts rather than education specialists or researchers, and based in teaching establishments not research centres, meant a grave shortage of initial expertise in evaluation.

Each project director planned the scale and style of evaluation appropriate to his situation, with varying degrees of advice from the Directorate and the independent evaluators. Evaluation was an important discussion topic at the several meetings and workshops organised for project staff but there was no attempt to impose a rigid methodological pattern. Rather these discussions, and others between projects and the Directorate, sought to ensure the Programme's evaluation needs were appreciated fully and that project directors were aware of the strengths, weaknesses and resource implications of the various techniques that might be used. Advice from the independent evaluators was similarly non-prescriptive in detail but was firm at the level of aims and general strategy; it exerted a strong influence on what was attempted. For example, the extensive evaluation undertaken by the MATLAB project at Napier College, Edinburgh, was wholly of the new-style, illuminative kind.

A central educational evaluation activity in projects was the developmental testing of material with sample students. Closely observed trials of new packages with a handful of students often stimulated major improvements in structure and presentation. Other less intense methods such as questionnaires were used to gain overall indications of student reactions to CAL as a whole and comments on specific materials. Group and individual interviews with students and staff were also used widely. Often the data gathered was little more than a global impression of the project and served only to suggest the general level of acceptance achieved.

The presence of independent financial evaluation forced a discipline on project staff which was initially alien and which they often found difficult to accept. Many projects instituted staff diaries as a means of collecting the time utilisation figures required. Funded staff found these rather a chore and academic staff sometimes refused point blank.

The Programme Committee

As well as being the primary audience for reports from the Directorate and independent evaluators, the Programme Committee made a few direct moves in the evaluation area. Occasionally a sub-committee was established to probe a project proposal on which a clear decision could not be made from the papers available. A sub-committee was established in 1976 to facilitate communication with the independent educational evaluators as a result of Programme Committee's unease with UNCAL's reports and style of evaluation.

A nominee of the Programme Committee, usually one of its members or a relevant member of Her Majesty's Inspectorate, served on each project's steering committee. For example, John Ounsted, HMI, the nominee to the Hertfordshire Computer Managed Mathematics Project (DP 2/02A), was a regular attender of steering committee meetings and through visits to participant schools kept closely in touch with progress. He made no secret of his doubts about certain aspects of the system and gave the project team much advice and criticism. The Scottish, Welsh and Northern Ireland Inspectorates performed a similar service to projects in their areas.

The Programme Committee nominee's role was especially important when midterm evaluation reports were presented to the Committee. Rarely was there any significant disagreement with the Director's report or recommendation regarding further funding but the nominee's first-hand reporting added a further perspective.

In the later stages of the Programme the Inspectorate played a part in the DES deliberations over arrangements necessary and desirable to support CAL post-77. Inspectors made a planned series of visits to projects and fed reports into the decision-making apparatus of the Department. Taken together their reports must have constituted a substantial body of evaluation evidence. It is interesting that when faced with the important task of rounding off the Programme and planning for possible continuation, the Department employed this established mechanism in addition to the Programme's extensive independent evaluation.

A theme of the Programme's approach to evaluation was the importance of personal experience; teachers and administrators were encouraged to see for themselves rather than accept written testimony. In this respect Programme Committee members' visits to projects were much appreciated by project staff.

Outcomes

The majority of the products of the Programme's evaluation efforts are openly available for scrutiny. They are also revealed in the quality and quantity of teaching materials and learning systems developed, and the understanding of the nature of CAL that has been created.

There is, however, one outcome from the Programme's evaluation which deserves special mention, namely the creation and identification of research potential. The relationship between research and evaluation and the part each should play in a development programme has been a continuing controversy. A review of CAL research in the United Kingdom highlights the point that the Programme's developmental aim of institutionalisation led it away from research to applications work; 'Had the Programme been designed to generate information relating to a clearly defined set of questions then a very different strategy might have been used' (Annett, 1975).

This distinction emphasises the important fact that the Programme and its evaluation work were not designed as CAL research and the information that was fed to decision-makers was not research evidence. Nevertheless, Annett (1975) was hopeful of 'questions which might be susceptible of more systematic investigation by a research oriented rather than development oriented programme' arising from the evaluators' probings of CAL in action. This has in fact happened and a number of projects are now formulating research proposals and looking for support.

Conclusion

The task of evaluation within the Programme was firstly to inform and facilitate management action by improving the data and perceptions available as a base for decisions; secondly to assist the drawing of conclusions and forming of generalisations. It made a qualitatively different contribution from that which formal research might have provided and made different demands of everyone concerned. Research would have placed a different type of information before decision-makers and suggested very different generalisations. Instead of the Programme's wide-ranging, subjectively based generalisations framed in everyday language, a research programme would almost certainly have yielded narrower, more objective generalisations couched in precise technical terms and limited by various reservations. Also if the Programme had engaged in research rather than concentrating on development there would be much less current use of CAL upon which to base generalisations and to see for oneself.

Thus the Programme's various evaluators should not be chided for failing to answer research questions; that was not their task. Judgement of of their success should depend on perception of the extent to which they have helped the creation of worthwhile CAL activity and improved its survival prospects through building a better general awareness of its attributes and costs.

References

ANNETT, J (1975) *Computer Assisted Learning 1969-1975*, Report for the Social Science Research Council

CRONBACH, L J (1975) 'Beyond the two disciplines of scientific psychology', *American Psychologist* 30, pp 116-127

FIELDEN, J (1974) 'The financial evaluation of computer assisted learning projects', *International Journal of Mathematical Education in Science and Technology* 5, 4, p 625-630

HARRE, R and SECORD, P F (1972) *The Explanation of Social Behaviour*, Oxford: Basil Blackwell

HOLLAND, J G (1961) 'Evaluating teaching machines and programs', *Teachers College Record,* **63**, 1, pp 56-65

HOOPER, R (1975) *Two Years On, The National Development Programme in Computer Assisted Learning, Report of the Director,* London: Council for Educational Technology

MACDONALD, B (1977) 'The educational evaluation of NDPCAL', *British Journal of Educational Technology* **8**, 3

MACDONALD, B, JENKINS, D, KEMMIS, S and TAWNEY, D (1975) *The Programme at Two*, University of East Anglia: Centre for Applied Research in Education

WRIGLEY, J (1976) 'How to assess innovation in schools' *New Society*, 8 July

8. Computing aspects

A continuing message throughout this final report is the diversity of CAL and CML activity, in contrast to the monolithic stereotype of 'computerised programmed learning'. Nowhere can this diversity be better illustrated than on the computing side of the National Programme.

The diverse computing environments of NDPCAL projects were, to some extent, the result of a funding strategy decision taken in the early months of 1973. In contrast to CAL funding in North America, the National Programme decided to spend as little as possible of its own funds on hardware, so as to release money for the all-important staffing required to create the software. Thus, the emphasis was to be on projects using, wherever possible, the wide range of existing and available computers. This strategy exacerbated the problems of transferability, and it attracted criticism from those who felt that, if NDPCAL did not buy computers, no useful development work could ever be done. But it fulfilled its main purpose: permitting a large amount of educational applications software to be written, tested and put into regular use with students.

The diversity of computing environments is illustrated in Figure 15. Projects within the National Programme used most makes of computer that are available to, and in, educational institutions. Large main-frames, 'midis', and BASIC-only 'minis' were all involved. As a general rule, CAL tends to run on the smaller, and CML on the larger, computers. Some of the computers were 'dedicated' to CAL or CML activity, others were general-purpose machines for scientific computing or local authority data processing. In contrast to the stereotype that CAL and CML are synonymous with interactive computing via terminals, all eight CML projects, the Imperial College mechanical engineers (DP 1/02A), and two out of the three schools CAL projects, used batch processing — with no significant problems of teacher acceptability. Indeed in the Hertfordshire Computer Managed Mathematics Project, terminals were dispensed with during the project because teachers found the batch system easier to use.

For the range of terminals used in the CAL projects see Figure 16. In setting up the Programme, the Government made a modification to the NCET recommendations of 1969: the development of a special terminal for educational use should *not* be pursued with NDPCAL funds (Hooper, 1974, pp 61-2). Three standard types of terminal were adopted — the

BURROUGHS	B5700; B6700
CDC	6400; Cyber 70, 76 and 7314
CTL	Modular One
DATA GENERAL	Nova 2; Nova 800; Nova 820A; Nova 840; Nova 1200
DIGITAL	PDP 8L; DEC System 10/50; PDP 11/10; PDP 11/40; DEC TSS/8
ELLIOTT	4130
GEC	4080
HEWLETT PACKARD	HP 2000E; HP 2000F; HP 2116C
IBM	1130; 370 range
ICL	4-70; 4-75; 1900 range; 2903
INTERDATA	7/32
NCR	Century 201
PRIME	300; 400
SIGMA	RXDS Sigma 9
UNIVAC	1108

Figure 15. Computers used by NDPCAL

MANUFACTURER	MODEL
CDC	713 Visual Display Unit
COMPUTEK	300 Graphics Visual Display Unit
DIGITAL	DEC VT52 Alphanumeric Visual Display Unit
IBM	3271 Visual Display Unit
KODE	ASR and KSR Teletypes
LYNWOOD	DAD and DAD-1 Visual Display Units
NEWBURY	21-40, 21-80, 7001, 7004 Visual Display Units
TEKTRONIX	4002A; 4006; 4006-1; 4010; 4010-1 Graphics Visual Display Units; Tek 611 Storage Tube
TELEPRINTER EQUIPMENT LTD	Terminet 1200
TEXAS INSTRUMENTS	Silent 700 Teletypes

Figure 16. Terminals used by NDPCAL

ubiquitous teletype, the visual display unit (VDU, called in North America a CRT, cathode ray tube), and the graphics terminal. To qualify the enthusiasm of those who assert that the cheap computer terminal is just round the corner, it is worth noting that in the years 1973-77 the UK sterling price of the Tektronix graphics terminals and the Kode Teletypes purchased by the Programme doubled.

The MATLAB graph function on a teletype

The size of computer programs developed by projects showed considerable diversity. As a general rule, by comparison to program sizes in commercial computing, NDPCAL's educational programs were small. One big exception to this was the CAMOL suite of programs, developed by International Computers Ltd (ICL) in collaboration with NDPCAL. CAMOL contains about 140,000 lines of COBOL programming. The size of individual CAL programs developed during the National Programme ranged from less than 100 lines of coding to over 6000, according to a survey carried out by John Peterson, production manager of the CALCHEM project (DP 1/06A). The typical size of CAL programs was somewhat greater than 400 lines; there were equal numbers of programs above and below this size. Much effort devoted to CAL programs was in those over 600 lines; less than 20% of effort (as measured by lines of coding) was in programs below this size (Peterson, 1977).

Finally, the diversity of computing environments was also reflected in the various projects' computing staff (what the Americans call 'liveware'). As was stated in the Director's first report, *Two Years On*, 'The Programme has found itself standing uneasily between the professional and the amateur, trying, inevitably, to get the best of both worlds' (Hooper, 1975, p 59). Some projects had access to highly experienced systems analysts from industry, others to inexperienced student programmers. Some programs were written by professional software houses under contract, others by teachers caught with the computing bug. If there was a common denominator, it was probably the comparative youth of the staff involved: 'the whole area (of CAL and CML) is still quite young, without a large body of associated experience, examples, or know-how' (Bevan, 1976, p 5).

Technical evaluation

The diversity of computing environments, in terms of hard-, soft- and liveware, made the task of technical evaluation difficult from the outset. Whereas financial and educational evaluation were contracted to independent agencies, technical evaluation was planned to be carried out by the Programme Directorate. There were a number of reasons for the Programme Directorate's difficulties with technical evaluation. For one thing, the criteria used in technical evaluation — computer efficiency, programmer productivity, etc — are not well established in the computing industry at large. 'There are no absolute standards of quality and efficiency in the computer world ... standards are subjective, context-dependent and "easier to recognise than to describe" ' (Bevan, 1976, p 16). If this is true of the computing industry, then how much more true is it of educational computing. The Directorate often found itself in the cross-fire between strongly conflicting views about computing issues, for example the transfer of author language programs. The views, expressed by experienced computing staff, often had a sectarian quality about them.

With a few exceptions, projects did not take kindly to the Directorate's technical evaluation. They saw it as dominated by paradigms more suited to commercial computing — prespecification of tasks, formal division of labour in the project team, adherence to national standards, elaborate documentation. The Directorate's technical evaluation should, in the view of the project staff, have taken more account of the reality of educational computing — pragmatic trial-and-error development due to inherent difficulties with prespecification, fluid combination of roles in project teams with one and the same person being systems analyst/programmer/operator when necessary, the inapplicability of national standards in the decentralised tradition of UK education, and 'functional' as distinct from 'bureaucratic' documentation.

Technical transferability

Early in 1973, Ken Knight of the University of Surrey suggested that hardware compatibility was really the only sensible route to technical transferability. This approach had been adopted in Scotland and France, for example, with the acquisition of compatible computers for computer education in secondary schools. Given the strategy decision outlined at the beginning of this chapter, hardware compatibility, however attractive an idea, was not possible. NDPCAL had by and large to live with what existed in educational and training institutions. Single-handed, the Programme could not, even with a much bigger budget, have turned back the tides of incompatible technology caused by the English educational tradition of decentralised decision-making, and computer manufacturers' vested interest in producing non-transferable software.

The problem of technical transferability was approached in four main ways.

1. Programming languages
2. Documentation
3. Design of programs
4. Maintenance and aftercare

1. Programming languages

In order to control the diversity, and increase chances of transferability, the Programme restricted the range of programming languages to be used by projects. Unlike the North American pattern, no NDPCAL funds were spent on producing new languages. As with computers and terminals, the emphasis was primarily on use of what already existed. Almost all the software for CAL was written in the two most widely available languages, BASIC and FORTRAN IV. For CML, which is close to commercial data processing applications, COBOL was favoured. Wherever possible, programming in assembly or machine language was avoided in favour of higher level languages. The major exception to these 'rules' was the Leeds Author Language (LAL) already well developed and operational at the University of Leeds by the time the National Programme began in 1973.

However, the decision to 'standardise' on high-level programming languages is a solution which brings new problems.

'. . . versions of one language differ from one producer to another and one compiler to another. Input, output and storage facilities will vary from one machine to another as may the operating system, even though the two basic machines may be given the same designation by the manufacturer. All factors are likely to change with time and are often subject to local alterations. Given such a fluid situation, there are few strategies for transfer that can be expected to achieve very much for very long. One is to confine all programming to a standard subset of a standard language, and implementations to a minimum core size and set of facilities. Unfortunately, any such sets would be so limited that programs would be clumsy and inefficient, and the educational experiences inevitably rather dull, and no advantage could be taken of improvements, in languages or hardware, because of invalidating all previous products. A more effective solution is to define a language and facility subset, and to include this set as part of a product's documentation. Deviations from this set can then be noted against the program listing, and references to facilities outside the set confined in given program areas. This procedure eases the process of transfer ... [and] has been adopted in relation to BASIC with a National Programme subset of the language' (Hooper, 1975, pp 60-61).

The transfer of teaching materials programmed in an author language tends to raise special problems, since most author language interpreters are very machine-dependent, often written in assembly language. Here again, there was conflict between some projects and the the Programme

Directorate, and continuing uncertainty as to the best policy. Early on, the Directorate put forward the view that author languages could by and large be dispensed with in favour of standard high level languages like BASIC or FORTRAN. A concerted critique of this stance from the author-language-using projects, notably CALCHEM and the Glasgow CAL group, led to a Directorate change of view. CALCHEM in addition rejected the Directorate assertion that author languages were difficult to transfer. To prove it, they wrote an 'interpreter' for a subset of the Leeds Author Language (in FORTRAN) called STAF (Science Teacher's Authoring Facility). The interpreter method of transfer of author languages was recommended to the Directorate in 1973 by Derek Sleeman, a computer scientist at the University of Leeds and was initially opposed by the Directorate. Derek Sleeman pointed out that the essential problem of producing an interpreter in a high level language for LAL would be the response time/core requirements of the interpreter. He suggested some simple experiments which would provide this data for the Directorate. By early 1977 STAF had been implemented on 9 makes of hardware at 17 sites in the UK and abroad (Peterson and Sessions, 1977). However, the STAF solution has its critics, and the Computer Based Learning Project (DP 1/01B) at Leeds is producing another interpreter for the complete Leeds Author Language, written in an assembly language (MINIMAL) to some people's surprise. Translators are written from MINIMAL to the assembly languages of standard machines, so that the host institution receives the interpreter written in its own assembly language.

2. Documentation

Given that quite a lot of CAL programs are small in size, making them 'portable' may not always be cost-effective, since they can be written again at the new site without much difficulty. This argument holds particularly in higher education but not so well for schools. If small programs are to be rewritten, proper documentation will greatly ease the process. For this reason, and to signal deviations from the standard language and facility subset (see above), documentation was emphasised as a transferability technique within the National Programme. The attempt was made to achieve a reasonable balance between over-elaborate documentation on the one hand and none at all on the other. In deciding on the level of staffing for projects at the design stage, the requirement for good documentation played an important role. Indeed, the use of NDPCAL funds to document programs, which is a time-consuming process, was positively favoured.

3. Design of programs

'A well designed, executed and versatile product will find a larger and more appreciative market than will a limited and poorly designed one' (NDPCAL, 1975, p 15). Given the lack of agreement within the industry generally about what constitutes good program design, and about the virtues of 'content-free' versus 'content-specific' software, emphasis on design considerations to ease transferability tended to remain exhortatory rather than specific. Within the Programme, certain topics of concern were identified and discussed, but these were never translated into formal guidelines. Good programming practice concerns itself with five main topics: 'ease of usage, ease of variation, reliability, efficiency of operation, cost-effectiveness' (Rymell, 1974, p 1). Thus for example, in Adrian Rymell's design of the 'context and content-free' CAMOL software, modular techniques were used. This enables the user to choose which program modules he wishes to implement in his context (discarding the others) and, just as important, enables the user to write his own context-specific modules, with a standard interface, which plug into the imported CAMOL modules. At Glasgow, in the maths and medical projects, Barry Scott's software design emphasised the separation of programs from data whenever possible, thus allowing the 'content-free' programs used for medical teaching to be transferred to new teaching contexts, for example in police training, and be filled with new data.

4. Maintenance and aftercare

Bob Lewis, the director of the Schools Council 'Computers in the Curriculum' project, and assistant director of the NDPCAL-funded CUSC project, emphasised early in the Programme's life the need to consider the problems of maintenance and aftercare if transferability is to happen systematically. Like documentation, maintenance and aftercare of developed programs tend not to be done with overmuch enthusiasm. Maintenance and aftercare will not happen 'naturally', they need to be organised and funded. It was with these objectives in mind, that the National Programme funded, for example, two program exchange services (GAPE and PSPE).

The British computer industry

In 1973, the Programme was asked by the Department of Industry, which served as one of the seven government departments on the Programme Committee, to 'make all reasonable attempts to use the products of, and develop links with, the British computer industry' (Hooper, 1975, p 18).

Two of the most active CAL centres in UK universities, Glasgow University and Leeds University, are using British computers (GEC 4080 and CTL Modular One, respectively). The leading project in advanced further education, at Napier College, Edinburgh, installed a CTL Modular One, with College and NDPCAL funds, to act as the centre of Napier's computing service both for computer science and CAL. At schools level, four of the five projects in CAL and CML used British computers (all ICL 1900 series). In military and industrial training, only two projects used British computers.

The National Programme kept close contacts with British computer manufacturers from the beginning — notably ICL, CTL and GEC Computers. The major cooperative development with British industry was the CAMOL project (Computer Assisted Management Of Learning).

Almost all the terminals funded by NDPCAL, or bought by project institutions with their own funds, were American. The only exceptions were the visual display units built by Newbury Labs. In the closing months of the Programme, however, a British-built graphics terminal was announced, the SIGMA Graphic Option Controller. CAL enthusiasts at the University of Surrey had made a large contribution to its development.

Conclusion

Based on the experience of the Programme, it must be reported that computing technology, both as regards hardware and systems software, is still very unreliable. Only a few of the projects escaped significant disruption of work caused by hardware and systems software faults. This was as true of American computers as of British computers. These disruptions were only minimised through the presence of skilled computing staff. Yet, paradoxically, a message coming out of the Programme is that the real difficulties surrounding CAL and CML are not primarily technical. What requires attention are the human, political, and educational environments. For this reason, both the Programme itself and most of its projects were not directed by computer specialists.

References

BEVAN, J D (1976) *Computing in NDPCAL*, Working Paper No 4, London: National Development Programme in Computer Assisted Learning

HOOPER, R (1974) 'The National Development Programme in Computer Assisted Learning — origins and starting-point', *Programmed Learning and Educational Technology* **11** 2, pp 59-73

HOOPER, R (1975) *Two Years On, The National Development Programme in Computer Assisted Learning: Report of the Director,* London: Council for Educational Technology

NDPCAL (1975) *Transferability in Computer Assisted and Computer Managed Learning.* Working Paper No 3, London: National Development Programme in Computer Assisted Learning

PETERSON, J W M (1977) 'The typical CAL program', *CALNEWS 8,* London: National Development Programme in Computer Assisted Learning

PETERSON, J W M and SESSIONS, A E (1977) 'A transportable authoring system', paper presented at the CAL 77 conference at the University of Surrey

RYMELL, A (1974) *Guidelines for the Systems and Programming Design of the Computer Managed Learning Project,* Working Paper No 1, London: National Development Programme in Computer Assisted Learning

9. How the money was spent

The way in which the National Programme's budget was spent highlights a number of interesting features of the work. The total expenditure in the period January 1973 to December 1977 was £2,592,665. Because this report was finalised in July 1977, the expenditure from April 1977 to December 1977 has had to be estimated. All other figures for financial years 1973/4, 1974/5, 1975/6, 1976/7, are taken from the audited accounts. The original budget of £2 millions, approved by the Secretary of State for Education and Science in the spring of 1972, was increased by 23% over the period due to inflation.

The size of the budget — the magic figure of £2 millions — had an important influence on the Programme. Simply put, it gave the Programme Directorate power to influence significantly the direction in which CAL was to travel. With a smaller budget, the Directorate would have had great difficulty in carrying through some of the more radical funding strategies — for example, the emphasis on inter-institutional projects. The size of the budget brought a certain status to the Programme, allowed it to command an audience within and beyond the funded projects, and ensured that people listened and responded to Programme ideas. The Programme Directorate's negotiating position with project institutions was a strong one. This was particularly important in 1973 when it was necessary to 'sell' the idea of development projects to universities familiar with the research grant philosophy.

Spending by financial years is set out in Figure 17. Of the total expenditure (£2.6 millions), £396,320 was spent on central administration (15%). The salaries of Directorate staff, office rent, and publications budget were the largest components. £198,540 was spent on independent educational and financial evaluation (8%). The remaining £2 millions (77%) was spent on projects. Even given the active role of the Directorate in policy-making and project management, it was felt important to keep central administration costs as low as possible, so that the maximum resources were available to fund activity in education and training institutions across the country. The battle for CAL and CML is won (or lost) amongst teachers.

Of the total expenditure of the Programme, £402,811 was spent on non-recurrent items (16%). By contrast, £1,647,604 was spent on staffing

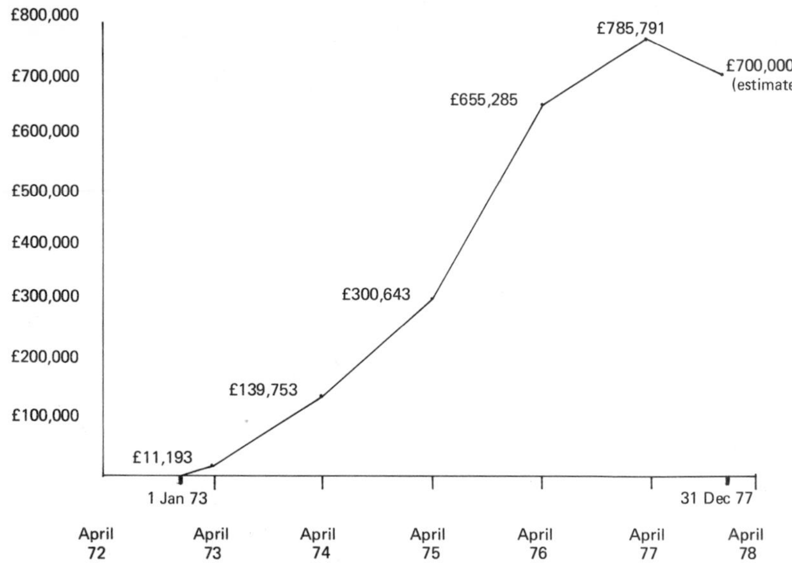

Figure 17. Total NDPCAL expenditure by financial years

(61%). At its peak, the Programme was funding over one hundred people.

Another strategy decision, with budgetary implications, was to encourage personal contact as the key to transfer. Given the Programme's emphasis on inter- and intra-project communication, and on dissemination to new adopters by word of mouth, live demonstrations and special exhibitions, it is rather surprising in fact how small the percentage of spending on travel and subsistence turns out to be in relation to total expenditure, £115,605 (4.5%).

Of the total expenditure on projects (£2 millions), tertiary education had by far the largest share at £1,249,822 (62.6%). This stems directly from the initial guidelines given to the Programme by the sponsoring Government departments in 1973. Figure 18 sets out the expenditure on projects, feasibility and design studies, by project category.

Finally, the NDPCAL budget of £2.6 millions was able to attract between £2 and 2.5 millions in 'matched funding'. Totals of matched funding are not precise and should be treated as estimates. It is important to note that not all matched funding was 'below the line' costs — eg, academic staff time. In the higher education projects, for example,

Tertiary education	£1,249,820	62.6%
Schools	402,670	20.2%
Armed Services	128,810	6.4%
Industrial training	106,380	5.3%
Transferability	109,430	5.5%
Totals	£1,997,110	100.0%

Figure 18. NDPCAL expenditure on projects, feasibility and design studies, by project category

dedicated computers for use on CAL were purchased with institutional money (Glasgow University, Surrey University, Queen Mary College). The CAMOL project involved International Computers Ltd in significant (6-figure) funding of the programming/documentation of the CAMOL programs. It is very unlikely that the strategy of 'matched funding' would have worked as well if the NDPCAL budget itself had been small in the first place. Money attracts money.

10. Strategy and performance — an assessment

In general, the various funding strategies evolved within the Programme to help achieve its aims seem to have proved effective. The existence of, and emphasis on, a wide-ranging evaluation allowed no serious errors of strategy to go undetected and uncorrected for long. However, on a number of occasions weaknesses were detected not so much in the strategies themselves but in how they were implemented, that is to say at the level of performance. Here it was more difficult to make improvements.

Development strategies

Cooperative funding

The cooperative funding policy, as reflected in the relationships between the London-based Programme Directorate and the various project staffs around the country and formalised in the use of 'matched funding', brought substantial benefits and some difficulties. The major benefit of cooperative funding seemed to be that it provided some solution to the problems associated with the 'centre-periphery' model of national curriculum projects, on the one hand, and the parochial research models on the other. Cooperative funding allowed projects to combine the advantages of 'centralisation' (increased transferability leading to cost reductions) with the advantages of 'localisation' (increased teacher participation leading to better institutionalisation). The cooperative approach allowed project directors to make significant contributions to the Programme's shape and philosophy, thus making the Programme (not just the projects) adaptive to changing views and circumstances.

The difficulties of the cooperative funding strategy were primarily human. The approach required people in the Directorate and in the projects to be able to give and take, to disagree without causing mutual resentment, to persuade rather than coerce, to see the other point of view, to be able to balance principles with pragmatism. The comparative security of 'them and us' funding, where the line between project proposers and project approvers is clearly drawn, was replaced by more ambiguous stances. The tensions implicit in cooperative funding were however usually counterbalanced by the cordial personal relationships which grew up between the Directorate and project staff.

In one or two projects, the Programme Directorate ran into difficulties when it moved away from the cooperative strategy and tried to 'impose' innovative uses of CAL and CML from outside on to an inadequate local base. Put conversely, the Programme Directorate achieved most success where it saw its role working alongside existing CAL/CML practitioners in given locales, helping to nurture, prune, fertilise organic growth.

Development time-scales

At both the level of strategy and performance, time-scales were continually problematic. The Programme consistently underestimated the time-scale required to get an adequate technical base for CAL/CML developments (equipment plus staffing) in those project institutions which did not already have such a base. It was difficult in projects to get computing time-scales to match educational development time-scales. On a number of occasions, computing developments got too far ahead of educational development, leading to expensive modifications, and, in one case, abandonment of the computing system.

Research and development

The relationship between research and development within projects was not always well-defined. The lack of any clear SSRC policy towards CAL research, combined with the Programme's aggressively stated developmental aims, led to research concerns (as distinct from evaluation concerns) being given low priority. The two least successful development projects in the Programme had the most explicit research bases. A reason for their failure to institutionalise was probably a confusion between research and development objectives. Some (not all) of the strongest projects in development terms had no relationship to educational research at all, and indeed were sceptical of its value.

Strategies to promote institutionalisation and transferability

The strategies for promoting institutionalisation and transferability in higher education were not necessarily applicable to other sectors of education and training. Taking institutionalisation in higher education, for example, the CAL practitioner is likely to be close to, if not actually involved in, the process of deciding the allocation of resources within the institution. Thus the Programme's model of 'collusive entrepreneurship' between Programme and project director worked well in higher education. But in schools, in further education, and in industrial training, the CAL practitioner may be a long way — geographically and in status terms — from the resource allocators. Thus the Programme had to develop in a more *ad hoc* manner models of entrepreneurship which brought together the three parties — the funding agency, the CAL practitioners, and the decision-makers. This involved a detailed local knowledge of widely varying contexts which the Programme Directorate did not always have. Success with institutionalisation in the military training projects was helped by the fact that NDPCAL's Assistant Director, Roger Miles, had previously worked in military training.

Matched funding

It was originally envisaged that the level of external funding to a project would decline over the five years as the level of matched funding increased. Mainly as a result of the worsening economic situation affecting all education, this did not happen in many projects (one place where it worked well was the Leeds statistics project). As a result the transition to institutionalisation — where matched funding takes over altogether — was more difficult. In a number of projects, a higher level of matched funding should have been insisted upon at the midterm evaluation point. With hindsight, the Directorate should not have been so ready to go on paying the full salary of some project directors out of National Programme funds (most project directors were academic staff funded locally), since this definitely weakened the chances of institutionalisation. On this general point, it can be argued that the Programme's strategy of funding people rather than hardware had a potentially harmful effect. It led to the possibility of teachers being 'spoilt' by the existence of skilled development staff who did most of the CAL development. In one higher education project, for example, of the 400 hours needed to produce the average CAL package, only 50 hours were recorded to have been contributed by academic staff, the rest coming from NDPCAL-funded staff. With less generous development staff funding, projects might possibly have been encouraged to produce materials in less labour-intensive ways. The harmful effects of generous staffing provision may become obvious after the Programme ends, if local budgets cannot find cash to keep some (obviously not all) specialist CAL staff on. Taking a pessimistic view, CAL development will swiftly decline given the unwillingness or inability of teaching staff to find more of their own time for it.

Tensions between institutionalisation and transferability

It was not recognised at the outset of the Programme that the twin aims of institutionalisation and transferability could on occasions be incompatible. The cultural and financial incentives in educational institutions tend to favour institutionalisation at the expense of transfer. Decision-makers — particularly at times of economic difficulty — need persuading that extra resources should go into making a local product transferable to other institutions. Some projects never successfully resolved the tension between the two aims and tended to fall between both stools.

Evaluation evaluated

Finally, at the risk of appearing unduly narcissistic, some assessment can be made of the Programme's widespread evaluation activities — particularly as they were carried out by the Directorate itself and the independent evaluators.

Programme Directorate

The main evaluation procedure designed by the Programme Directorate — the midterm evaluation — stimulated a distinct increase in productivity and encouraged careful documentation of project experience. The opportunity to rehearse arguments for convincing outside audiences was a useful side benefit. The main benefit, however, was that it did reveal, in many cases, exactly what mid-course corrections were needed. Most projects seemed satisfied that the procedure had been thorough but fair, and protests were confined to specific details or the severity of individual criticisms, rather than disputing the overall outcome.

The major failing of the Programme Directorate was in technical evaluation — both as regards strategy and performance. As the CALCHEM project wrote in its final review report: 'we have commented before on the lack of useful guidance on computing matters and must again indicate our regret that the major national programme in CAL should not have a more authoritative voice in matters of computing systems and languages for CAL. We feel that we have learned the hard way and lost a lot of time in so doing : we hope that others may not need to follow the same stony path through lack of knowledge or guidance' (Ayscough, 1977).

Two other weaknesses in the Directorate's own evaluation activities should be noted. More could have been done to search out the critics of CAL, to track down the dissident voice rather than listen to the converted. On occasion the Directorate felt itself constrained from doing so out of loyalty to relevant projects (this is the disadvantage of building the Programme on cordial personal relationships).

Secondly, the Directorate had particular difficulties with the whole question of cost-effectiveness. By having two independent evaluation agencies, one to look at costs and one at educational effects, and by funding most activity in education rather than in training, the cost-effectiveness issue tended to get left out. However, in defence, it needs to be said that cost-effectiveness evaluation in education raises methodological problems. Also the Programme consciously invested most of its energies in those applications of the computer which *did not* duplicate the functions of other media, thus comparisions between CAL and traditional teaching were largely inappropriate. Resources would have been invested in cost-effectiveness studies if the Programme Directorate could have been convinced that cost-effectiveness data directly influence education's adoption of innovation.

The independent evaluations

The independent evaluations — particularly UNCAL's educational evaluation — caused more debate and disagreement than any other single feature of the Programme. A major reason for this was the fact that both UNCAL and John Fielden developed and refined novel methodologies to handle the evaluation problems thrown up by the Programme.

The two evaluation methodologies proved overall to be resilient and appropriate. The real problems with the independent evaluations, most notably UNCAL, were at the level of performance rather than strategy. Whilst the Programme Directorate and the majority of projects benefited enormously from UNCAL's advice and insights, UNCAL has to date failed to reach one of its own main targets, to get information across to decision-makers such as the Programme Committee, and to the wider lay public outside NDPCAL. The style, and length, of some UNCAL reports made them difficult to understand. UNCAL always seemed most at home writing for other evaluators. Striving to satisfy academic criteria, UNCAL sometimes lost sight of practical necessities. Tending to concentrate on studying and reporting the methodological problems of the evaluation *process*, UNCAL did not always serve the needs of decision-makers for evaluation *results*.

Fielden's performance was consistently successful with decision-makers. His reports were always read by Programme Committee members, for example. There were occasions, however, when the financial evaluators presented their results in a way which invited inappropriate direct comparisions between CAL and conventional methods of teaching.

Also some of the data used, for example the apportionment of academic staff time, had low credibility.

Both evaluation agencies had difficulties keeping up with the size and pace of the Programme. The higher education projects, for example, got detailed attention whilst other sectors were in danger of being neglected.

Conclusion

The wide range of strategies adopted by the Programme turned out, overall, to be appropriate to the development aims of the Programme. Whether the procedures and ideas set out in these chapters would be appropriate to a funding agency involved exclusively in research, is not certain. Whilst there is much overlap (not to say confusion) between research and development, they are different activities. The National Programme was concerned with a 'practical' activity in Schwab's meaning of the word: 'By the "practical" I mean a complex discipline, relatively unfamiliar to the academic and differing radically from the disciplines of the theoretic. It is the discipline concerned with choice and action, in contrast with the theoretic, which is concerned with knowledge' (Schwab, 1969).

References

AYSCOUGH, P (1977) *CALCHEM: Final Review Report*, Department of Chemistry, The University of Leeds

SCHWAB, J J (1969) 'The practical: a language for curriculum', *School Review,* **78**, 1

PART FOUR

THE FUTURE

Second aim of the National Programme: 'to make recommendations to appropriate agencies in the public and private sectors concerning possible future levels and types of investment in computer assisted and computer managed learning in education and training'.

11. CAL and CML in education — the next ten years: a report and recommendations to Government

Introduction

In 1976 and 1977, a future study was carried out to fulfil the second aim of the Programme: 'to make recommendations to appropriate agencies in the public and private sectors concerning possible future levels and types of investment in computer assisted and computer managed learning in education and training'.

The outcome of the study was a series of specialised reports tailored for different audiences. This chapter on education, and the following chapter on training, contain the report and recommendations to appropriate central Government departments. In addition there are four individual reports available, for higher education institutions, local authorities, military and industrial training agencies, and two specialist reports on computer managed learning, and technological trends in the 1980s (details of these reports are found in Appendix C).

Methodology

The methodology chosen for the future study was straightforward. A series of background papers was commissioned, which attempted to identify relevant social, economic, educational and technological trends to 1990. Six working parties were set up, with membership drawn from people in and outside the Programme, to identify likely and desirable trends in computer assisted and computer managed learning. In addition, literature searches were carried out, and contact with overseas agencies was made.

Difficulties encountered

The future study was a complex, often frustrating, task. It was difficult, for example, to keep predictive statements (what *will* happen) separate from prescriptive statements (what *should* happen). Much of the extensive future study literature in education turns out to be a thinly veiled attack on current educational practice and an opportunity to draw up radical future 'scenarios' containing the authors' highly personal value judgements.

It proved impossible in practice to meet the aim of recommending 'possible future levels' of investment in CAL and CML, for three reasons. First of all, current levels of investment in CAL and CML are not identifiable within aggregated budgets, thus a recommendation that higher education, for example, should allocate £x millions to CAL would be of doubtful value. (However, the report on higher education does indicate the level of funds likely to be needed for a particular institution to introduce a viable CAL service). Secondly, the current and future sums involved in CAL and CML are likely to be small in relation to total educational spending, although, of course, *overall* costs of computing in education (which includes research, administrative applications, and computer education/science) are and will be more significant. Thirdly, statements about possible future levels of national investment in CAL and CML might in some senses run counter to a central recommendation coming out of the study. This recommendation (see below) argues against blanket provision of CAL/CML facilities.

Another difficulty with the future study arose out of the desire to tailor reports and recommendations to the various agencies receiving them. Many of the existing future studies seem to have been written under no such constraint. Much of the content that is normally associated with a future study report ended up, to use an analogy from film-making, on the cutting room floor. There is no point in discussing at length, and recommending, a course of action to an agency which has no executive influence over that action (unless of course that agency is predicted to change its sphere of influence). For example, the Government departments dealing with education in the United Kingdom have very few powers over what goes on in the classroom: 'central education government is *responsive* rather than either controlling or initiating' (Halsey, 1976, p 191). Thus, this chapter does not talk in terms of a 'national CAL policy' and restricts itself largely to those issues where Government is likely to be (or chooses to be) influential. Similarly, the report to local authorities was written in the knowledge that local authorities also have limited (some would say, very limited) control over their educational institutions in such matters as the introduction of educational computing.

Computers in education — here to stay

The main conclusion to come out of the future study is obvious, yet needs to be stated. Computer assisted and computer managed learning are becoming established in educational institutions from secondary school to university, both here in the UK and abroad. The major question facing decision-makers is not therefore *whether* this should happen, but *how*.

A steady and evolutionary growth is seen as both likely *and* desirable. Investment should be planned to happen gradually, in relation to finances available, user demand and proficiency, the nature of particular academic disciplines, and the changing technology. Blanket provision of facilities across institutions and subject disciplines would be wasteful and unproductive.

Higher education is likely to retain its leadership in the development and regular use of CAL and CML over the next ten years, with secondary and further education moving more slowly. A major reason for this is the continuing unreliability of the computing technology which requires the presence of skilled computing staff. Such staff will always be more available in higher education institutions.

The major benefit from computer managed learning will be to assist the move to resource-based and individualised learning. 'Steady growth of resource-based learning' is predicted (Becher, 1976, p 9). The major benefits to come from investment in computer assisted learning are likely to be qualitative in nature — teaching new topics that could not be taught with existing methods, assisting in the teaching of 'higher order' skills such as decision-making and problem-solving, and improving the quality of existing teaching by tailoring it more sensitively to the individual needs of the active learner. Both CAL and CML could contribute to a solution of 'the central paradox that is likely to characterise teaching and learning in the 1980s. Though teaching and learning are likely to be more open and flexible, they are also likely to demand a far closer and more precise system of guidance and assessment for both students and teachers than heretofore' (Eggleston, 1976, p 15).

Add-on cost

A major problem associated with the growth of computer assisted and computer managed learning will, in the foreseeable future, remain cost. Whilst a dramatic decline in the hardware costs (notably storage and CPU) and some possible decline in telecommunications costs are predicted (Knight, 1977; Owen, 1976), the software costs to produce good teaching materials with the computer show no signs of reduction. Indeed, software costs will increase, because software is and will remain labour-intensive, because more sophisticated terminals (involving graphics capability) will be used in education, because more sophisticated models of the subject matter, pedagogy, and learner will be incorporated into teaching programs, and because computer manufacturers will increasingly realise more of their income from software to offset declining income from hardware. One type of computer assisted learning, where the student writes his own computer programs in specially designed languages like LOGO to explore particular problems (Howe, 1976), may as a result grow faster than other types which depend on programs being prewritten by teachers. The claims regularly made that author languages will reduce software costs because they are 'easy to use' seem, in the Programme's experience, much overstated.

There is a temptation to believe that the high cost of CAL and CML applications can be offset by reductions in other parts of the educational budget, for example, teachers and laboratory equipment. A decade of experience in the UK and 15 years' experience in the USA would suggest that this is not possible (although it is possible in training — see next chapter). CAL and CML are add-on costs to the budget, requiring additional staff and resources. In this respect, CAL and CML are, of course no different to language and science laboratories, audio-visual aids and educational television.

Versatility

There are four characteristics of the computer which reinforce its future importance within education. Firstly, it is a versatile technology, with uses ranging widely across many areas of academic research, administrative applications, and growing uses in the classroom. Teaching applications of the computer have, contrary to widespread belief, very varied educational objectives — the computer as object of instruction, as tool of the disciplines, as means of individualised instruction. Thus, the base of support for computing in education is broad, rather than narrow.

One of the versatilities of the computer, particularly important for improving acceptability in an educational setting, is the fact that software can be modified to suit local conditions. By contrast to the fixed format of the medium of educational film, the computer provides the teacher with a resource which can be adapted to suit his or her particular tastes.

Respectability

The second important characteristic of the computer in education is its 'academic respectability'. Computing should not be viewed as just another audio-visual aid (though this is indeed one legitimate way it is used in the classroom). Computing is becoming, and this will increase over the next decade, *indistinguishable* from the fabric of a widening range of academic

Hertfordshire Computer Managed Mathematics Project: a pupil checks work from the computer printout

Class work with the Hertfordshire Computer Managed Mathematics Project

disciplines (maths to social history to art and design). It has been argued, for example, that physics may be entering a period which will see a reduced emphasis on the calculus in favour of algorithms and numerical approaches (Hinton, 1977). Such a transition, which will be opposed by the classical Newtonian physicists familiar with analytical problem-solving, has obvious implications for computer assisted learning. The relationship of computing to academic disciplines, and therefore to the teaching of them, has many similarities with the relationship between print and the disciplines. In universities, for example, the costs of computing (3.9% of total spending) are catching up fast on the costs of libraries (4.9%), whilst only 0.5% goes on audio-visual services (Pearson, 1977). But of course, libraries themselves are becoming increasingly dependent on computing technology for the ever more complex tasks of information retrieval. Publishing is also becoming computer-dependent. The high costs of scholarly publishing are forcing people to consider alternative methods such as electronic publishing. Thus computing and print are merging, making computing yet more academically indispensable.

Simulation

Thirdly, the computer derives power from its abilities as a simulator. Simulation, well established for many years in training, would seem to be becoming an increasingly powerful tool in education. In the years ahead, the curriculum in many subjects will reduce the traditional emphasis on content and factual transmission for which CAL is not a cost-effective medium anyway, in favour of problem-solving skills for which CAL seems well suited.

A world industry

Finally, and most significant of all in the 1980s, computing in education will be affected in ways we cannot properly imagine by computing's fast growing status in world industry and dominant role in communications and control applications. Computing occupies a key position in what has been called 'the second industrial revolution' — from wheels to electrons, from brawn to brain. The so-called 'information industries', which are increasingly dependent on computing and telecommunications, now account for more than 20% of the US Gross National Product and are predicted by 1980 to employ half the labour force of the country (Program on Information Resources Policy, 1976, pp 4-5). As a result of these

A CAL tutorial in the Computational Physics Teaching Laboratory at Surrey University

trends, which are accelerating, computing developments within education will be given firm political support. Such support will be linked with continuing demands on education to respond imaginatively to the country's industrial/vocational requirements.

Recommendations to Government

The Government, principally the Department of Education and Science, is in a position to influence three important matters over the next decade:

1. dissemination of CAL and CML
2. provision of educational computing facilities
3. new developments.

1. Dissemination

If there is to be a continuing emphasis on dissemination and transferability following the end of the National Programme in 1977, central government finance will be required. It is recommended that such financing be made available, and that any dissemination agencies set up with government support should be expected to become self-financing within three to five years. By the mid-1980s, it is likely (see below) that dissemination will be made easier by the fact that routine commercial publication of CAL, CML materials will be feasible. At the moment the market is not yet sufficiently large.

A three-tier structure for the dissemination of CAL and CML within the UK is recommended. The top two tiers will require central government funding. There is a requirement, first of all, for a small UK-wide agency, preferably located within the Council for Educational Technology, to carry on from NDPCAL and act as a focal point for information and consultancy, to coordinate continuing activity, to market CAL materials and experience at home, to operate a central index of all relevant computer-based materials, and to establish where appropriate national standards for CAL work. Within three years, this central unit should merge into CET's overall policy and activity.

Secondly, there is a requirement for a network of subject-based program/information exchange agencies, based on the prototypes funded by NDPCAL. These agencies may best be based in educational institutions with development experience and continuing commitment. The work of each agency is likely to involve teacher training, marketing, consultancy, some low-cost development, as well as the operation of a library. By the early 1980s, if not before, the library operation should be self-financing and the requirement for teacher training and consultancy reduced. The decision to recommend subject-based agencies comes from a desire to exploit teachers' existing communication channels, which are primarily subject-affiliated.

Thirdly, at the local or regional level, there already exist (and more are coming into being) information and program library services for users in the catchment area of particular computing facilities. These educational computing services, which cover the range of subjects appropriate to their users, do not require direct central government funding. In the reports to higher education institutions and local authorities, emphasis is laid on the need to set up, as demand and finance warrant it, a coordinated service for computer assisted learning and educational computing (NDPCAL, 1977a; NDPCAL, 1977b).

2. Provision of educational computing facilities

Historically, central government has played a significant role in decisions concerning the provision of computing facilities for educational institutions. It is recommended that this role be clarified in the university sector, and strengthened outside. Whilst the provision of educational computing facilities as a whole is not within the remit of NDPCAL, CAL often shares the same facilities with research and computer science applications. It is for this reason that a recommendation concerning overall provision of computing facilities is included here.

In the university sector, as demands for computer assisted learning facilities grow, there is likely to be a need to clarify the division of responsibilities between the Computer Board and the University Grants Committee. There is a danger that CAL within teaching departments, which tends not to be a Computer Board concern, will develop in an *ad hoc* manner, unrelated to CAL activity within university computing services, over which the Board does have influence. The miniaturisation, thus declining cost, of computer technology will exacerbate this issue over the next few years. Given the Board's history of commitment to, and success with, resource-sharing between universities, it would be helpful if the Board had overall care of CAL funding.

Outside the university sector, the way in which educational computing facilities are currently planned, approved and provided is not likely to be adequate to future demands. Some coordination is provided through the Department of Education and Science's consideration of proposals for computer purchases under the FE Regulations and the informal advice provided by Her Majesty's Inspectorate. But this coordination is necessarily limited because the arrangements rely on dealing with individual proposals as and when they arise. The Computer Board is able, for example, to negotiate for universities lower prices for software and hardware, whilst other educational institutions, with much less finance available for computing cannot benefit, ironically, from any such collective mechanism.

It is suggested, as a matter of some urgency, that the Department of Education and Science examine the way in which educational computing facilities in England and Wales outside the university sector are planned, approved and provided, with a view to adopting a more coordinated approach possibly along the lines of the Computer Board. It is realised that this suggestion could lead to some realignment of powers between central and local government in favour of central government. Such a realignment for a specialised purpose is not, on present evidence, thought to be out of the question.

There are four main reasons for examining provision of facilities. First of all, the limited finances likely to be available in the next few years could be made to go further. Secondly, the swift technological changes, notably to do with miniaturisation, increase the likelihood of *ad hoc* provision, with a possible proliferation of incompatible small machines in separate institutions, where larger, shared machines might possibly be more cost-effective. Thirdly, education would benefit from being able to speak with a more unified voice to the computer manufacturers. At the moment, there is no effective mechanism for communicating educational requirements to the industry. Fourthly, the growth of computer networks is likely to demand careful national and regional standardisation if they are to be utilised cost-effectively.

3. New developments

The third area where the Government can choose to exert its influence is in the direct funding of new developments in computer assisted and computer managed learning. The high costs of new development mean that, in general, it will not in the near future happen 'naturally'. In the period 1978-80, given the economic constraints, new development funding should not command high priority. Indeed the three-year period after the end of the National Programme will provide a valuable opportunity to test the real strength and acceptability of the CAL/CML 'movement', which began with SSRC and Nuffield funding at the end of the 1960s and was then liberally fertilised by the National Programme from 1973-77.

In the early 1980s, however, given more favourable economic conditions (Oxford Analytica Ltd, 1976), and less pressure of numbers on education (Williams, 1977), a second wave of new development funding merits active consideration. A major reason for planning further development in the early 1980s is to prevent the impetus and reservoir of talent created by the National Programme being dissipated. Impetus and talent, which are central to any innovative activity, are expensive to re-establish once lost.

A number of candidates for new development funding in the 1980s suggest themselves. Given that the present interest in continuing education for adults grows rather than falters, and given the likelihood of widespread adoption of home terminals probably along the lines of the Post Office's Viewdata scheme, significant opportunities will arise to develop CAL and CML for home-based distance teaching. Educational broadcasting in the UK has developed fastest outside formal educational institutions, and there is no reason why the same pattern might not happen with computer assisted learning. The US Carnegie Commission's influential report on instructional technology predicted: 'Although traditional institutions may employ the new technologies for 10 to 20 per cent of their instruction by the year 2000, extramural education may use them for up to 80 per cent of their instruction' (The Carnegie Commission on Higher Education, 1972, p 52).

Other areas ripe for development include the teaching of the handicapped (Howe, 1976; Morris, 1976). In West Germany and North America, substantial progress has been made with computer assisted learning techniques in special education.

In addition, there are likely to be a number of useful technological objectives in any second development programme. New software techniques will need to be created, with the aim of increasing software productivity (Knight, 1977). Computer networks, in full-scale operation for research purposes by the 1980s, and new types of stand-alone terminal (notably for graphics), will both need to be investigated and tried out in teaching.

By the mid-1980s, it is likely that the development of teaching materials for the computer can become commercially viable, as with today's textbooks and films. At this point, a new problem will arise which will be a further good reason for Government activity in the early 1980s. When CAL and CML go fully commercial, there is a real danger of US manufacturers dominating the world market — for hardware, software and experience.

In the late 1960s, American firms saw, prematurely as it turned out, a commercial market for computer assisted instruction. In the late 1970s, US firms are re-entering that market, with greater caution. Significant development activity, funded by the British Government, with well established links to British industry (both the manufacturers and the software houses), would ensure that world markets, and the British classroom, did not become an American monopoly.

Conclusion

In summary, no revolutions for computer assisted and computer managed learning in education are predicted *or* prescribed. A period of gradual and sustained growth is required, geared to finances available, teacher commitment, changing curricula and changing technology. Neither natural growth by itself, nor at the other extreme, large scale development by central fiat, are recommended. The strength of CAL and CML has indeed been its organic growth. But that growth needs to be pruned and fertilised at particular points, and this is a task for central and local government.

Given the 'constitution' of the British educational system, and the very small amounts of cash in the large educational budget which are available for innovative development, there are real limits to the control that central government, vice-chancellors and local education authorities, can exercise over what goes on in teaching and learning. Yet without judicious control, educational computing will suffer. Faced with a rapidly growing world industry aggressively marketing its products, educational purchasers could in the 1980s become, in the words of a local authority official at an NDPCAL presentation, 'lambs to the slaughter'.

References

BECHER, R A (1976) *Higher Education in the Eighties,* commissioned paper for the NDPCAL Future Study

CARNEGIE COMMISSION ON HIGHER EDUCATION (1972) *The Fourth Revolution — Instructional Technology in Higher Education,* New York: McGraw-Hill

EGGLESTON, J (1976) *Developing Patterns of Teaching and Learning in Schools*, commissioned paper for the NDPCAL Future Study

HALSEY, A H (1976) *Tenth Report from the Expenditure Committee,* memorandum by Dr A H Halsey to the Fookes Sub-Committee on 'Policy making in the Department of Education and Science', London: HMSO

HINTON, T (1977) 'The Assimilation of CAL within a Department', paper presented at the CAL 77 Conference at the University of Surrey

HOWE, J A M (1976) *AI and CAI Ten Years On,* commissioned paper for the NDPCAL Future Study to be published in *Programmed Learning and Educational Technology* **15**, 2, May 1978

KNIGHT, K R (ed) (1977) *TechnologiCAL. A Future Study Report*, Technical Report No 17, London: National Development Programme in Computer Assisted Learning

MORRIS, J G (1976) *Education in the Next Decade and the Use of Computers for Learning*, commissioned paper for the NDPCAL Future Study

NDPCAL (1977a) *Computer Assisted Learning in Higher Education — the Next Ten Years. A Future Study Report*, Technical Report No 14, London: National Development Programme in Computer Assisted Learning

NDPCAL (1977b) *Educational Computing in the Local Authority Sector — the Next Ten Years. A Future Study Report*, Technical Report No 15, London: National Development Programme in Computer Assisted Learning

OWEN, K (1976) *Trends in Computing to 1990*, commissioned paper for the NDPCAL Future Study, published as appendix to NDPCAL Technical Report No 17, London: National Development Programme in Computer Assisted Learning

OXFORD ANALYTICA LTD (1976) *Education in Britain — Demand and Supply to 1990: The Economic Background*, commissioned paper for the NDPCAL Future Study

PEARSON, P K (1977) *Costs of Education in the United Kingdom*, commissioned paper for the NDPCAL Future Study, London: Council for Educational Technology

PROGRAM ON INFORMATION RESOURCES POLICY (1976) *Information Resources Policy: Arenas, Players and Stakes*, Annual Report 1975-6, Volume One, Harvard University

WILLIAMS, G L (1976) *A Forecast of Pupil and Student Numbers 1975-1990*, commissioned paper for the NDPCAL Future Study

12. CAL and CML in training — the next ten years: a report and recommendations to Government

This chapter on the future of computer assisted and computer managed learning in industrial and military training in the United Kingdom draws heavily on two future study reports written by Roger Miles, *Computers in Industrial Training and Management Development in the 1980s* and *Computers in Military Training in the 1980s* (Miles, 1977a; Miles, 1977b), The primary audiences for these two reports, and for this chapter, are the Training Services Agency and the Ministry of Defence respectively. In the case of industrial training, a range of other agencies, for example industrial training boards, is also addressed.

Industrial training and management development

With the exception of computer-based simulators, CAL is as yet a minor activity and low priority in industrial training circles. Unless there is a dramatic change in the present situation, the 1980s will find industrial training lagging far behind education and military training in computer applications. A number of factors seem to have hindered the application of computers to industrial training. Their identification is important because there are good grounds for believing that computers could and should play a more important part in industrial training in the future.

Factors inhibiting CAL developments in training

Industrial training is a heterogeneous area, not a coherent entity. A great many widely differing groups require and use different training systems which often operate in small isolated groups. Therefore any innovation cannot spread easily or rapidly without authority and resources to support promotional effort.

A great many other things have been happening in industrial training during the last 10-15 years when CAL has been evolving from a research interest into a practical reality. The 1964 Industrial Training Act, for example, was a major innovation to command attention.

There has been a growth in the use of training packages and a rapid expansion in the range of relatively cheap audio-visual aids readily available to trainers with money to spend. In comparison to such aids, computers are expensive and more effort is required to master them. Few training departments have had the computing expertise even to know where to begin.

Commercial interests, such as the pressure for immediate results and minimum costs and the need for secrecy about products and processes, do not create a supportive environment for innovative research and development or the sharing of results.

Some of the early proponents of the tutorial style of CAL made claims to be able to improve learning and replace teachers which are now recognised as having been grossly exaggerated. These extravagant claims could have aroused a negative reaction among instructors who have heard them all before in relation to teaching machines and programmed learning.

Likely training needs in the 1980s

Plans to exploit the computer's potential as a training aid in the 1980s must obviously be based on an assessment of future training needs and computing facilities likely to be available.

The developing pattern of employment could create opportunities for CAL. For example, more and more people will be involved in information-handling jobs which will increasingly involve working with computers. Many existing jobs will become computer-related as computerisation spreads, and more opportunities for CAL methods will occur.

Given rapid changes in employment structure, the work force will need to be flexible and where possible develop generalisable skills. 'Higher order' planning and problem-solving skills will become more important in many jobs and the emphasis of training will move away from procedural and manipulative skills. There are indications that CAL methods could provide the realism, complexity and individual adaptivity desirable when training for these higher order skills.

Automation and increasingly sophisticated technology will bring important changes in manufacturing and production industries. There will be a growing demand for maintenance and process-control skills, areas where CAL is showing its potential in current trials. The higher cost of automated systems and inaccessibility of components will create training problems for which computer simulation provides a solution.

The challenge to management of these occupational changes and other pressures, will make management development even more important. CAL can help to create increased realism in management development activities and could be a means of bringing training to managers in their offices in response to the growing demand for in-company training.

Manpower at all levels will become more and more expensive. Training systems which develop individual abilities fully, provide course content which is relevant to the particular trainee, and which quickly react to weaknesses in trainee's background and skills, will be needed. The military and educational experience with computer managed learning (CML) demonstrates how the computer can improve diagnostic assessment and facilitate better, more responsive course management.

Computing facilities

One thing is certain — the continued rapid growth of the computer industry. In particular, there will be a growth of on-line systems with remote terminals linked to large central processors. A number of companies, for example British Airways, have shown it is both feasible and cost-effective to develop 'piggy-back' uses of these on-line systems for training. There will also be increased use of mini-computers within companies. These may offer more flexibility than the larger systems because of being under local control. Whilst 'piggy-back' uses of existing computing facilities for training are likely to be favoured in the short term, in the longer term it will be necessary for training to obtain its own 'dedicated' facilities if CAL does grow to any size. Increasingly in the future, computer manufacturers will be vigorously marketing CAL systems for use in industrial training.

Resource implications

It is important to recognise that, like many training innovations, CAL and CML are rarely a straight replacement for existing methods. The new method frequently introduces opportunities to attack new aims and achieve different outcomes. Thus a direct comparison of the cost of old and new methods may be misleading

The initial cost of CAL is likely to be higher than for most other training aids, thus cooperative development amongst users will increase the chances of economies of scale. Equipment is only part (and a diminishing one) of the total cost. Computing is by no means a transparent technology and potential CAL users will need professional staff to plan, install and operate systems. Also development of the teaching material calls for considerable effort; experience has shown that the ease with which instructors can use an 'author language' to write CAL tutorial programs is often exaggerated.

Claims that CAL can replace instructors should be treated with caution. Usually, the computer is an aid to the teacher, taking over some functions and releasing time for others, but also creating new tasks. It is important to see the computer as a powerful addition to the available range of instructional resources, which complements the others including the teacher. The benefits of CAL and CML will come from a variety of contributions to training but wholesale replacement of instructors will not be one of them.

On present evidence it appears that computers can make valuable contributions to industrial training as follows:

(a) by replacing some of the expensive, complex equipment in technical, maintenance and operator training — simulation can be cheaper and safer, and can also give more extensive experience of the system being simulated
(b) by improving course management procedures, especially testing and record-keeping functions
(c) by making individualised courses easier to operate and reducing overall course length
(d) by enabling more effective on-the-job training to be given, thus reducing the expense of travel to, and accommodation at, residential courses
(e) by enabling large, geographically spread-out organisations to standardise and swiftly update training that is administered locally.

Recommendations

The recommendations which follow are for those decision-makers with national responsibilities for training and management development. The recommendations are premised on two beliefs:

(a) CAL and CML have something worthwhile to offer industrial training in the 1980s; they are feasible and could be cost-effective
(b) CAL and CML will not be taken up without substantial energising and directing effort by relevant authorities.

A comprehensive CAL information service for industrial training should be established. It should be an authoritative, impartial agency competent to advise prospective purchasers of computer systems.

A program exchange facility for business and commercial subjects should be established, to minimise development costs by encouraging more utilisation of available CAL programs and coordinating creation of new materials.

The industrial training boards and other training coordinating authorities should be encouraged to develop the expertise needed to identify, promote and assist appropriate CAL applications in their areas of training.

The existing experience base is small, and generalising from education or military training will not locate potential benefits of CAL which are unique to industrial training or management development. Therefore a programme of CAL research and development specific to these areas needs to be mounted.

Military training

National Programme funding of six feasibility studies and two development projects has enabled the Armed Services to broaden their experience of computer applications to military training and expand existing work. Without doubt the major use of computers in military training continues to be within simulators, but a range of activities in which the computer aids teaching and learning has been developed. Interest in the computer as an aid to course scheduling and management of training has been particularly strong and should lead to further applications in the future. Also one of the Programme-funded projects, in computer assisted electronic fault-finding training at RAF Locking, has aroused great interest as a potentially very cost-effective use of computers in training. These priorities are reflected in the recommendations which resulted from the future study.

Compared with the very substantial use of CAL and CML by the US Armed Forces, the British military applications are on a much smaller scale and generally at an earlier stage. Furthermore, there are important differences between the American and British military training systems which cast doubt on the suitability of some of the American methods for British requirements. Nevertheless the future study found much of interest in the American experience, which underlined the need to keep in close contact with developments in the US Armed Forces and elsewhere.

Military tasks and training

In the early 1980s the effects of the Defence Review of 1975 will still be

A CAL graphics package in use at the Royal Naval College, Greenwich

working through the Services. That review made large economies through a major reorganisation of the defence system; changes which will affect training significantly and so have important implications for computer applications.

In fulfilling its commitment to the Western Alliance, Britain provides forces for all 3 elements of NATO's strategy, conventional forces, theatre nuclear forces and strategic nuclear forces. Thus Service personnel will continue to require the full range of military skills for effective defence against conventional and nuclear forces. Severe limitations on personnel and resources will make the quality and speed of training more important than ever.

The advanced military equipments to be used in the 1980s will demand high levels of operator and maintenance skill to utilise their sophisticated facilities and increased power. There will be a shift in emphasis, as in industrial training, from manipulative repair skills to fault-finding and diagnostic abilities. As weapons and communications equipment become more sophisticated there will be a growing requirement for special-to-type training, even where the operational equipment is only used in small numbers. Also it will be difficult to use operational equipment for training without jeopardising its readiness. The computer's ability to generate inexpensive 'software' simulations could be valuable for these training needs.

Training organisation

Within each of the three Services there will be pressure for rationalisation and centralisation of training facilities. The current method whereby the managers, maintainers and operators of a system may be trained in different locations could be replaced by training at one location where adequate simulation and real equipment can be provided.

Centralisation into large training centres dramatically complicates the scheduling problem and even with computer help it may be difficult to utilise resources smoothly and economically. Rationalisation of training into fewer locations could make important savings on resources and buildings but managing the increased number of trainees at any one place would be much more difficult. An important factor to be considered is the need to keep the maximum number of personnel operational at any one time; decentralised training methods, which bring training to the operational unit instead of men returning to schools, could assist the attainment of this objective. Computers could be one important means of delivering well designed on-the-job training, particularly for those working on the increasing number of equipment systems which incorporate computers.

Manpower factors

The number of 18-year-olds is going to decline dramatically, reducing from 925,000 in 1982 to 783,000 in 1989 and by 1992, it could be as low as 647,000. Thus the pool for recruiting will be reduced and the Services can expect strong competition from higher education and industry. If it becomes necessary to relax recruiting standards yet maintain or, given the increasingly sophisticated equipment, even improve training performance, then flexible training adaptive to individual needs will be required. Computer managed learning methods could be helpful in organising and monitoring such training.

An important trend in the 1980s could be the shortening of engagements which will have a major effect on patterns of training and employment. A growth of modular training to prepare men for specific tasks rather than longer career courses could increase the need for pre-structured material including CAL. It is noticeable in the polytechnic sector of education that modular course structures have led to an increase in the use of computers for management and administration.

Recommendations

The first requirement for exploiting the potential of computers in military training is to formulate a policy and create the organisational structures necessary for its implementation. Some allocation of resources specifically for this purpose will be needed if the longer term benefits are to be obtained. Much could be achieved by extending and adjusting the functions of existing training, computing and research organisations. However, some changes do seem necessary. For example, the present arrangements for procurement of major data processing systems seem inappropriate for some training applications, particularly pilot studies of innovations. For a variety of reasons, provision of small dedicated machines and systems in training establishments will be preferable to large centralised processors, for most applications. Nevertheless, central coordination will be needed to establish priorities, assess proposed applications and avert wasteful duplication of development effort. In the next few years, as training demands and computer technology change, arrangements for monitoring and evaluating new developments in CAL will be needed, including those applications pioneered by the US Armed Forces.

It seems clear that computer assisted learning work in Service higher education and advanced technical training is established and expanding. The main need in this area is for more cooperation and communication of experience to spread development costs. The value of CAL at these advanced levels of training relates to its ability to facilitate learning rather than reduce training costs. Yet it should be done as economically as possible.

At the lower levels of training, where CAL has made much less impact to date in the UK Armed Services, three priorities are suggested. Firstly, CAL systems incorporating software simulation offer a useful and cost-effective alternative to real equipment for aspects of maintenance training. Secondly, important savings in training resources may result from use of computer assisted course scheduling and resource management systems. Thirdly, computer managed learning systems can assist quality control in training, thereby improving the throughput of trainees, and take over clerical and routine functions.

As regards the growing use of computer-based simulation, there is a need to increase the contribution of training expertise to the design, use and evaluation of simulators. CAL/CML developments in the military sector have tended to be separate from developments with computer-based simulators. A coherent policy towards all computer applications in training would be more productive, especially since it is likely that computer-based simulators will incorporate some of the characteristics of CAL/CML systems (for example, diagnostic information about the trainee).

In summary, the following six recommendations are offered for consideration by training authorities in the Armed Services.

1. The centres of instructional technology expertise in each Service should be tasked with:
(a) providing advice and assistance on appropriate developments in CAL
(b) conducting necessary trials of new approaches.

2. Within each Service there is a need to clarify the sponsorship, procurement and funding arrangements for the creation and operation of computer applications to training.

3. In view of the high cost of research and development in this area there is an urgent need to ensure good cooperation and dissemination of

information on a tri-service basis. This should include systematic monitoring of activities in the USA and elsewhere.

4. Arrangements should be made to ensure the training effectiveness of all simulators by involving training expertise in the design process from the Staff Requirement stage, by providing training for all simulator instructors and by applying appropriate evaluation procedures.

5. All staff involved in training should be made aware of the scope, benefits and limitations of computer applications to training.

6. Particular areas for CAL development are:

(a) computer based training systems, with tutorial and simulation elements, for maintenance training

(b) computer managed learning systems, in close association with advances in instructional technology, to create better student assessment and course management procedures

(c) course scheduling systems and similar administrative applications.

References

MILES, R (1977a) *Computers in Industrial Training and Management Development in the 1980s. A Future Study Report*, Technical Report No 19, London: National Development Programme in Computer Assisted Learning

MILES, R (1977b) *Computers in military training in the 1980s. A Future Study Report,* Technical Report No 18, London: National Development Programme in Computer Assisted Learning

Epilogue

This final report concludes on a happy note. In July 1977 the Government agreed to make funds available to the Council for Educational Technology to enable it to undertake the task of disseminating and coordinating computer assisted and computer managed learning after the National Programme closes in December 1977. Funds will be made available to CET for a period of four financial years (1978/79 - 1981/2) on a gradually reducing basis. The grant in the first year will total £60,000.

The aftercare structure likely to be adopted by CET will include a small central unit in CET's London offices, plus a number of program exchange centres in various parts of the country. Users and potential users of CAL and CML will have access to general information and advice not necessarily related to particular programs or packages. Provision of this service will reduce unnecessary duplication of activity and will make generally available the experience gained in the Programme. The service will not include, however, provision for the funding of new development.

It is appropriate to end with a list of thanks to the many different people who helped to make the Programme such an enjoyable and productive enterprise.

From the beginning, the members of the executive Programme Committee were supportive and trusting. Programme Committee meetings, under John Hudson's Chairmanship, were always well attended and, on many occasions, debates were lively.

The permanent officials of Schools Branch III in the Department of Education and Science protected in difficult times the Programme's annual budgets from the colder economic winds and always found time to help with matters of policy and protocol.

Many members of Her Majesty's Inspectorate in England, Wales, Scotland and Northern Ireland were active, both on Programme Committee and on project steering committees, evaluating plans and people and giving the Programme access to a wealth of experience.

Within the Council for Educational Technology, Geoffrey Hubbard, the Director, acted as father confessor and consultant on many occasions. Norman Willis was of particular assistance on the publications side. Freddie Russell and Eric Smyth laboured to prepare budgets and pay project claims.

The external assessors, drawn from outside the Programme, made lively and penetrating contributions to the midterm evaluation visits.

The independent evaluators stimulated much good thinking in the Programme, and were responsible for spreading a climate of evaluation awareness. Despite some temptation, they kept their independence intact. The existence of friendly relationships between the evaluators and the Programme Directorate was not allowed to soften the critical comments that passed from time to time in both directions.

The many project and academic staff around the country were without doubt the powerhouse of the Programme. Project directors supported the Programme's aims with whole-hearted commitment and were a pleasure to work with.

Finally, thanks to my splendid staff on the fifth floor of the United Artists' building in Mortimer Street, London W1. Mrs Jill Frewin and John Bevan devoted their time to the complex computing aspects of the Programme, and were responsible for encouraging a sense of professionalism. The Information Officer, Mrs Ingrid Toye, gave the Programme a personal touch and a practical flavour. She combined the roles of walking reference library, PR officer, newsletter editor, graphics designer, marketing/copyright specialist and conference organiser. Kathy O'Neill, Sandra Crapper, Mrs Helen Roberts (née Richardson) put up with mountains of typing and project administration. In between times they were cooks, bottle-washers, waitresses, evaluators, conference guides, chauffeuses. Helen, who came with me from the BBC to found the Programme, sat skilfully and ever-smiling at the base of the National Programme grapevine, passing information and admonition up and down with the greatest discretion. Last of all, my thanks to Roger Miles: I could not have had a better Assistant Director.

Further information

Any enquiries about the National Programme, its projects and its publications may be addressed to

The Information Officer,
Council for Educational Technology,
3 Devonshire Street,
London W1N 2BA

Tel: 01-580 7553/4 or 01-636 4186

Appendix A: Membership of Programme Committee

Department of Education and Science
Mr J A Hudson CB (Chairman)
Mr R H Bird
Mr A E D Chamier
Mr F Makin HMI
Mr M Edmundson HMI

Scottish Education Department
Mr J G Morris HMI

Welsh Education Office
Mr Glyn Evans HMI

Department of Education for Northern Ireland
Mr N Morrison HMI

Ministry of Defence
Air Commodore H A Probert MBE

Department of Employment
Mr S J Dalziel

Department of Industry
Mr B R Taylor

Council for Educational Technology
Sir Brynmor Jones

Schools Council
Mr P J Dines

Social Science Research Council
Mrs A Pope

University Grants Committee
Miss B Naylor

Coopted members
Professor J Annett
Department of Psychology
University of Warwick

Dr G K S Browning
Director
The Computing Service
University of Glasgow

Mr G M A Harrison
Chief Education Officer
City of Sheffield

Professor K W Keohane
Rector
Roehampton Institute of Higher Education

Mr H A Randall
Managing Director
ESL (Bristol) Ltd

Dr A A L Reid
Head
Long Range Studies Division
Post Office

Mr L G Turner
Manager
User Training
National Computer Centre Ltd

Ex officio members
Mr G Hubbard
Director
CET

Mr R Hooper
Director
NDPCAL

Secretariat, Department of Education and Science
Mr B L Baish
Mr D H Padgett
Mr N J Cornwell

Appendix B: Summaries of funded projects and studies

DP 1/01B *Computer Based Learning Project* (*CBLP*)

Director: J R Hartley, MA, Computer Based Learning Project, Leeds University, Leeds LS2 9JT, Yorkshire. Tel: 0532 31751 x 7106

A computer-based statistics service course has been developed and is now in regular use with approximately 850 students from ten different social science disciplines in three institutions (the University of Leeds, Leeds Polytechnic and the University of Bradford). The Leeds Modular One computer with 56 terminals is used in a variety of ways. First, as a statistical laboratory, providing illustrations of statistical concepts, and calculation facilities; second, for providing individualised teaching of concepts and guidance in problem-solving and experimental design. The computer is also used as an interactive example bank. Much of the statistics course is taught conventionally in lectures and tutorials, using a series of Student Guides specially developed by the Project team. The materials are now fully integrated in the statistics teaching of departments, and are organised and managed by the lecturers and students themselves. A machine independent version of the Leeds Author Language has been written so that materials in applied statistics and chemistry (DP 1/06A) can be readily transferred.

Funded for 2 years from 1 October 1973 at a cost of £98,694.
Extended for 1 year from 1 October 1975 at a cost of £35,334.
Extended for 1 year from 1 October 1976 at a cost of £20,860.

DP 1/02A *Engineering Sciences Project* (*ESP*)

Director: Dr P R Smith, BSc, PhD, FINucE, FInstP. Faculty of Engineering, Computer Assisted Teaching Unit, Queen Mary College, Mile End Road, London E1 4NS. Tel: 01-980 4811 x 547

Many engineering systems are too complex and/or too costly to be made available for student experimental work, but system responses can be studied using a realistic computer simulation. Initially the project involved nuclear, mechanical and electrical engineering at QMC, mechanical engineering at Imperial College, and electrical engineering at University College London. Three other institutions have joined the project — Exeter University, Plymouth Polytechnic, City of Leicester Polytechnic. Links have also been established with two military projects (DP 3/01 and DP 3/02). A wide range of CAL packages has been developed and tested, and is now in routine use in a range of engineering courses. The transferability of packages has been a key objective, so as to spread the high development costs across different institutions.

Funded for 2 years from 1 October 1973 at a cost of £50,355.
Extended for 2 years 3 months from 1 October 1975 at a cost of £173,721.

DP 1/03A *Computational Physics Teaching Laboratory* (*CPTL*)

Director: Professor D Jackson, DSc, FInstP, Dept of Physics, University of Surrey, Guildford, Surrey. Tel: 0483 71281

A mini-computer is being used in a time-shared service to provide a computational physics teaching laboratory for use as an integral part of the honours degree physics course at Surrey. CPTL is used both in maths teaching for physicists and physics teaching. 70% of the academic staff in the physics department are involved in the work. Some physics tutorials take place within the laboratory, using packages developed by staff members. Students can investigate a range of physics problems and experiments, using numerical approaches. A library of teaching programs, some imported from other institutions, for example Cambridge University, is available for use by students and staff. The course material together with associated programs and operating instructions is now being disseminated to other institutions. (The mini-computer housed in the physics department is also being used by Development Project 1/09).

Funded for 2 years from 1 October 1973 at a cost of £21,040.
Extended for 2 years from 1 October 1975 at a cost of £28,240.

DP 1/04A *Clinical Decision Making*

Director: Dr C D Forbes, MB, ChB, MD, FRCP, The University of Glasgow, Dept of Medicine, Royal Infirmary, 36 Castle Street, Glasgow G4. Tel: 041 552 3535 x 532

A long-term objective of this work is to produce integrated courses in clinical decision-making for fourth- and fifth-year clinical medicine and general practice, involving bedside teaching, computer assisted tutorials in small groups and individual learning at terminals. The computer enables the clinical student to think about his own decision-making process. Computer-based materials are being produced for patient management problems (clinical medicine and general practice), and emergency situations, for example a car accident. In the patient management problems, students, often working in small groups around one terminal with no teacher present, can compare their decisions with the decisions of experienced doctors. In the emergency situation, students work against the clock to diagnose a given patient's condition. The medical work at Glasgow is part of a developing CAL service within the University, involving also maths and physics teaching (see DP 1/10).

The Department of Medicine, University of Leeds, has been associated with the development work. The Glasgow materials are being transferred to the Modular One computer at the University of Leeds and are being re-written in the Leeds Author Language. The Glasgow materials, modified for use with a Newbury 7004 terminal, are being transferred to the Medical School, Ninewells Hospital, University of Dundee.

Funded for 1 year 2 months from 1 April 1974 at a cost of £11,305.
Extended for 2 years 7 months from 1 June 1975 at a cost of £63,300.

DP 1/06A *Computer Assisted Learning in Chemistry* (*CALCHEM*)

Director: Professor P B Ayscough, MA, PhD, ScD, CChem, FRIC, Dept of Physical Chemistry, The University of Leeds, Leeds LS2 9JT. Tel: 0532 31751 x 6089

CALCHEM began as a cooperative of nine institutions in higher education, developing computer assisted learning materials for use in theoretical and experimental chemistry courses, with production teams of chemists and programmers based at Leeds University and Sheffield City Polytechnic. By 1977 the project involved 20 institutions of higher education in the UK and abroad, 100 chemistry teachers and 2200 students.

About 40 packages containing computer programs and ancillary material have been produced. The programs, mainly written in the STAF author language, have been implemented on most major computing systems.

The computer is used as a means of enabling students — on an individual basis — to study in a systematic manner the factors involved in the design of laboratory experiments, the interpretation of spectra, the solution of theoretical problems of various kinds, and the evaluation of experimental data. The major use of the computer is in tutorial mode, with complementary uses of the computer as a calculation and simulation facility.

Funded for 2 years from 1 April 1974 at a cost of £53,936.
Extended for 1 year 9 months from April 1976 at a cost of £91,050.

DP 1/07 (FS 1/01) *The MATLAB Project*

Director: D Leach, BSc, FIMA, MBCS, MInstP, Dean, Faculty of Science, Napier College of Commerce and Technology, Colinton Road, Edinburgh EH10 5DT. Tel: 031 447 7070

The requirement for a computer-based approach to the teaching of service course mathematics to students of HNC and HND in Engineering and SHND in Business Studies was examined at Napier College and Falkirk College of Technology in the initial feasibility study. A suite of programs called MATLAB ('*mat*hematical *lab*oratory') was developed to provide students with a mathematical and statistical laboratory, available through a simple mathematically oriented interface language. MATLAB consists of a variety of mathematical, statistical, and numerical techniques for solving problems. Traditional mathematics service courses in the project institutions are being altered by reducing the time spent on calculation and the techniques of mathematics, thus giving the student and teacher greater freedom to tackle engineering or business problems that require mathematical thinking. Emphasis has shifted from arithmetic to mathematical problem-posing and problem-interpretation. Paisley College of Technology, a Scottish Central Institution, has joined Napier and Falkirk in the design and use of MATLAB.

Funded for 1 year 5 months from 1 December 1973 at a cost of £12,558. Extended for 2 years 5 months from 1 July 1975 at a cost of £126,468.

DP 1/08 (FS 1/22/01) *CAMOL in Secondary and Tertiary Education*

Director: H McMahon, BSc, MEd, The Education Centre, The New University of Ulster, Coleraine, Co Londonderry, Northern Ireland. Tel: 0265 4141 x 341

The project in Northern Ireland continues the work begun in Feasibility Study 1/22/01. Based in the Education Centre of the New University of Ulster, the project is applying computer managed learning techniques to courses within NUU and within other educational institutions in Ulster. The computer software, CAMOL (*C*omputer *A*ssisted *M*anagement *O*f *L*earning) has been developed by a team from ICL (see TP 22/02B). In association with the project, the Physics Department of the Methodist College Belfast is producing an individualised A-level physics course to be managed by CAMOL, and Ulster College is studying the applications of CAMOL to the problem of academic administration. This project is linked with three other CAMOL feasibility studies, FS 1/22/03A at Brighton Polytechnic, FS 1/22/04 at Bradford College and FS 3/22/02 at Catterick.

Funded for 1 year 4 months from 1 August 1974 at a cost of £21,593. Extended for 2 years from 1 December 1975 at a cost of £92,272.

DP 1/09 (FS 1/04) *Computers in the Undergraduate Science Curriculum (CUSC)*

Director: Dr J McKenzie, MA, PhD, Dept of Physics and Astronomy, University College London, Gower Street, London WC1 6BT. Tel: 01-387 7050 x 490

CUSC is a large, inter-institutional and inter-disciplinary project, involving some 50 academic staff and 13 science departments in three institutions — University College London, Chelsea College and the University of Surrey. The aims of the project are to generate, develop, test and transfer CAL packages that enrich learning within the undergraduate science curriculum; to further the integration of such packages into existing science courses; and to investigate the role of CAL in science education. The computer's main use is for simulation, enabling the science student to focus his attention on the way a physical, biological or chemical system reacts to change of parameters. An important part of the project's work is to exploit the use of graphics terminals in teaching. A range of packages has been developed and tested for use in physics, biology and chemistry teaching at undergraduate level. A fourth institution, Queen Elizabeth College, is now participating in the work of CUSC.

Funded for 2 years from 1 January 1974 at a cost of £71,795.
Extended for 2 years from 1 January 1976 at a cost of £146,664.

DP 1/10 (FS 1/02A) *Basic Mathematics at Undergraduate Level*

Director: Professor J Hunter, MA, PhD, FIMA, University of Glasgow, Mathematics Building, Glasgow G12 8QW. Tel: 041 339 8855 x 7178

After an initial examination of the requirements for computer-based teaching materials in the area of mathematics service courses for 500 first-year undergraduates at Glasgow, the project aims to produce integrated courses for first-year university, college and sixth-form classes in Basic Mathematics using lectures, tutorials, texts and CAL modules. The main idea is to exploit as far as possible the parameters in the various parts of mathematics covered, in order to produce a dynamic situation rather than a static preselected one. The computer is used to give the student individualised practice of mathematical concepts introduced in lectures. 'Standard' errors are recognised and helpful comments are built in to try to encourage precision of thinking and presentation. Prompts of various kinds, often visual, are used to try to stimulate reaction. Branching preserves flexibility in appropriate places. To ensure consistency in the use of mathematical notation, and to assist in the teaching of geometry, graphics terminals are being used. The work in mathematics has now spread into physics teaching, as part of the developing CAL service within the University. Physics students are provided with tutorial help for a selection of examples, the help being available to them on a cafeteria basis. The mathematics teaching materials are now being transferred for use in Aberdeen College of Education.

Funded for 1 year 3 months from 1 January 1974 at a cost of £17,874.
Extended for 1 year 3 months from 1 April 1975 at a cost of £22,509.
Extended for 1 year 5 months from 1 July 1976 at a cost of £41,867.

DP 1/11 *Computer Assisted Learning — A University Service*

Director: T F Goodwin, CEng, FBCS(Hon), MRAeS, Computing Unit, University of Surrey, Guildford, Surrey GU2 5XH. Tel: 0483 71281

This project is concerned with establishing a centrally managed university-wide service for CAL at Surrey University. It is intended to build on the success of the University's two existing NDPCAL projects (the Computational Physics Teaching Laboratory DP 1/03A and Computers in the Undergraduate Science Curriculum DP 1/09), and on CAL activities already developing outside these projects, for example in the Dept of Mathematics. A library is being set up and advice on program writing and transferability provided. The service is financed in conjunction with the Computer Board and the University. The Computer Board has funded a mini computer dedicated to CAL work.

Funded for 1 year 3 months from 1 October 1976 at a cost of £7032.

FS 1/22/03A *Assessment of Student Performance and Progress*

Director: R C Stanley, BSc, Brighton Polytechnic, Moulsecoomb, Brighton BN2 4GJ. Tel: 0273 693655

This study aims to assist teaching staff at Brighton Polytechnic in the testing and assessment of student performance on modular degree courses, and to provide students with feedback on their own progress. It also aims to create conditions under which the facilities of the 'content-free' computer management software CAMOL produced in Transferability Project 22/02B, are taken up by staff in a range of courses in the Polytechnic. The study is linked with three other CAMOL projects, DP 1/08 at the New University of Ulster, FS 1/22/04 at Bradford College and FS 3/22/02 at Catterick.

Funded for 1 year 8 months from 8 September 1975 at a cost of £18,830. Extended for 7 months from 7 May 1977 at a cost of £6060.

FS 1/22/04 *CAMOL in Further Education*

Director: E E Robinson, MSc, Bradford College, Great Horton Road, Bradford BD7 1AY. Tel: 0274 34844

This study is centred at Bradford College, with the participation of Keighley Technical College and Shipley College of Further Education. Within Bradford College, there has been considerable research into and development of special teaching in mathematics for craft-level students of below average ability and attainment. This uses commercially available individualised material which, although of high quality, has not been satisfactorily validated for craft level students, and also poses management problems for the lecturers and students. The CAMOL system produced in the Transferability Project 22/02B is being applied to this learning system to examine the extent to which these problems can be alleviated. This study is linked with three other CAMOL projects, DP 1/08 at the New University of Ulster, FS 1/22/03A at Brighton Polytechnic and FS 3/22/02 at Catterick.

Funded for 1 year 3 months from 1 October 1976 at a cost of £12,440.

DP 2/02A *Hertfordshire Computer Managed Mathematics Project (HCMMP)*

Director: Dr W Tagg, PhD, MBCS, Advisory Unit for Computer Based Education, Hertfordshire County Council, 19 St Albans Road, Hatfield, Herts AL10 0HU. Tel: Hatfield (07072) 66121

A computer managed course for mixed ability mathematics classes in the first two years of the comprehensive school has been developed and is now in regular use in 12 secondary schools in Hertfordshire with 3000 pupils, and, in addition, 3 schools in the Inner London Education Authority. The course makes use of carefully structured individualised worksheets in addition to live teaching and the use of videotaped materials. The primary tasks of the computer are to mark worksheets and keep pupil records. All the schools use the system via batch processing and a courier service. The computer also generates, for off-line use, arithmetic exercises tailored to individual children's performance.

Funded for 2 years from 1 October 1973 at a cost of £56,838.
Extended for 2 years from 1 September 1975 at a cost of £85,507.

DP 2/03A *Computer Assisted Teaching of Remedial Reading*

Director: H Lloyd, County of South Glamorgan, Education Offices, Kingsway, Cardiff CF1 4JG. Tel: 0222 31033

Following design studies funded by NDPCAL, a computer managed system of teaching remedial reading using a wide range of commercially available and locally produced curriculum materials was produced and piloted with 380 children from 5 junior schools in South Glamorgan. One school made use of a terminal, the other four worked in batch mode. The system was intended to form the basis of a programme of remedial reading for junior school children with the intention of reducing the number of pupils who need special remedial treatment after the age of 11. The specially developed curriculum material is still in use, but the computer side of the work has not proved successful in South Glamorgan and has been suspended. From the material produced, a resource bank has been developed which is being used in South Glamorgan.

Funded for 2 years 3 months from 1 October 1974 at a cost of £110,549.
Extended for 8 months from 1 January 1977 at a cost of £5600.

DP 2/04 *Computer Assisted School Timetabling* (*CAST*)

Director: H Screen, Local Authorities Management Services and Computer Committee (LAMSAC), 3 Buckingham Gate, London SW1E 6JH. Tel: 01-828 2333

LAMSAC is evaluating the effectiveness of three existing commercial computer timetabling systems (NORDATA, OSA and SPL) and assessing the potential for extending the computer's contribution to good timetabling practice. An advisory service and information source on computer assisted timetabling for local education authorities is planned.

Funded for 2 years from 1 January 1976 at a cost of £41,087.

DP 2/05 (FS 2/02A) *The Local History Classroom Project* (*LHCP*)

Director: B D C Labbett, MA, County Hall, Ipswich, Suffolk. Tel: 0473 55801

The project based in Suffolk, arising out of a previous design and feasibility study, is involved in the creation and use of a computerised data base, holding 19th century census returns for selected Suffolk villages and towns. The data base has been used as a resource in the teaching of local history in 15 Suffolk schools and in adult education. The Metropolitan Borough of Dudley is cooperating with Suffolk in the development work. The approach is now being considered by secondary schools in four other local authorities. The emphasis of the work is on active participation by teachers *and* pupils in the development and use of the data base. An important end product of the classroom work is a series of 'Writing History' bulletins, containing work done by teachers and pupils at participating schools. The computer is used exclusively in batch processing mode, with the ICL information retrieval package FIND.

Funded for 1 year 1 month from 1 December 1974 at a cost of £15,748.
Extended for 1 year from 1 January 1976 at a cost of £8889.
Extended for 1 year from 1 January 1976 at a cost of £17,410.

FS 2/01 *Local Information Services Project (LISP)*

Director: L A Gilbert, Council for Educational Technology, 3 Devonshire Street, London W1N 2BA. Tel: 01-580 7553/4

This feasibility study had as its aim the investigation of the range of local information services which could be provided to teachers and pupils about book and non-book learning resources, through the manipulation by local computers of a nationally organised and locally augmented data base. During the year's work, two national film library data bases were implemented on a pilot basis on four local computers — Oxfordshire, Leeds, Clwyd and the New University of Ulster. ICL information retrieval software (MARC and FIND), suitably adapted by Southampton University, was used. A small number of trial searches was successfully carried out by the four operators. On the basis of the pilot work, it seems beyond doubt that the computer will, sooner or later, have a worthwhile role to play in the provision of information services about learning resources. Since the end of the NDPCAL feasibility study, CET has undertaken a major investigation with the British Library of the development of a national cataloguing and information service for audio-visual materials — a necessary prerequisite for any further activity.

Funded for 1 year from 1 January 1974 at a cost of £2261.

FS 2/03 *Computer Assisted Learning in Upper School Geography (CALUSG)*

Director: R J Robinson, MA, School of Education, University of Birmingham, PO Box 363, Birmingham B15 2TT. Tel: 021 472 1301 x 2289

The feasibility study aims to assist modern geography teaching in the sixth form by providing information and structured exercise material on specific topics, ideas, models or theories. The computer's main function is as a data storage and retrieval facility offering a variety of geographical information including simple maps. It is also being used to analyse and present data in various ways. 300 pupils and teachers from 11 schools representing some half dozen LEAs are involved in the design and trial of materials. The teaching materials produced can be used in the classroom with *or without* access to computers.

Funded for 2 years from 1 January 1976 at a cost of £39,904.

FS 2/04 *CAL in Secondary School History*

Contact on historical matters: Mr A R Worrall, or Mr J H Collins, Flint High School, Maeshyfryd, Flint, Clwyd. Tel: 03526 3296

Contact on computing matters: Mr P Weston, Kelsterton College of Technology, Connah's Quay, Deeside, Clwyd. Tel: Chester (0244) 817531

Following a design study carried out by NDPCAL, this feasibility study, based in Clwyd, investigated uses of the computer as an information retrieval device in the teaching of history, complementing the continuing work in Suffolk (DP 2/05). The computer can be used in three ways. Firstly, it stores references, suitably cross-indexed, to available learning resources on history topics selected by Clwyd teachers. Secondly, the computer stores a collection of statements from primary and secondary sources about the selected topics. A retrieval system allows teachers and pupils to make a range of on-line enquiries using the existing Clwyd time-shared computing system. Thirdly, the computer is used to store and manipulate nineteenth century census returns as part of the teaching of local history.

Funded for 1 year from 1 January 1976 at a cost of £11,946.

DP 3/01 *Computer Assisted Technological Education of Service Personnel* (*CATESP*)

Project base: Dept of Electrical and Electronic Engineering, Royal Military College of Science (RMCS), Shrivenham, Swindon, Wilts.

CAL packages enable students of electrical engineering to develop, exercise and test their knowledge of topics introduced in lectures and gain introductory experience of computer aided design. Six packages have been produced, 3 are under development and several others will be transferred from the Engineering Sciences Project. Three student stations, each comprising a graphics terminal and alphanumeric VDU, are available in a laboratory linked to the Department's PDP 11/40. Students normally work in pairs. Videotapes of computer generated displays are used for class demonstrations of system response characteristics and sensitivity to parameter changes. There is a possibility of expansion into other subject matter areas and departments with the establishment of a college-wide CAL service.

Funded for 2 years from 1 December 1975 at a cost of £24,879.

DP 3/02 *Computer Assisted Learning in Nuclear Science and Technology*

Project base: Department of Nuclear Science and Technology, Royal Naval College, Greenwich, London SE10 9NN.

The College has developed a number of CAL activities over the last few years and this project is expanding that work, in particular by introducing the use of computer based teaching packages. Some of the packages developed at Queen Mary College (DP 1/02A) are being transferred to Greenwich and three others on nuclear engineering topics are being developed locally. The project is also investigating further the use of the computer for analysis of laboratory-generated data and modelling of complex physical systems for design studies. The Department's facilities were enhanced early in 1977 by the installation of a PRIME 400 computer.

Funded for 2 years from 1 January 1976 at a cost of £9575.

FS 3/01A *Computer Scheduling of REME Training*

Study contractor: Dr M A H Dempster, PhD, FIMA, Oxford Systems Associates Limited (OSA), Balliol College, Oxford OX1 3BJ. Tel: 0865 47757

Study base: School of Electrical and Mechanical Engineering (SEME), Bordon, Hants

This study explored the feasibility of a computer solution to the problems of scheduling courses for a large REME training establishment. To meet the SEME requirement at Bordon, extensive improvements and changes were made to an existing package for 'job-shop scheduling' developed by Oxford Systems Associates Limited. Trials of the resulting system showed that a computer solution was feasible but MOD (Army) were not convinced of the new system's superiority over existing manual methods. Further development may be undertaken following a general review of the requirements of the scheduling task and work in this area.

Funded for 1 year 6 months from 1 January 1975 at a cost of £24,532. Extended for 4 months from 1 September 1976 at a cost of £7776.

FS 3/01B *Computer Aided Planning and Scheduling*

Study Contractor: Dr M A H Dempster, PhD, FIMA, Oxford Systems Associates Limited (OSA), Balliol College, Oxford OX1 3BJ. Tel: 0865 47757

Study Base: No 1 Radio School, RAF Locking

The general aim of this study is to design and implement a computer aided system for planning and scheduling the training programme at No 1 Radio School RAF Locking, with a view to optimising the allocation of training resources. The study is providing RAF Locking with assistance from OSA Ltd, in two stages, building upon earlier work by RAF Locking staff. Initially OSA will assist the design of a management system for the existing data base and provide an algorithm to manipulate it. In the second stage OSA will modify and install their system (see FS 3/01A) for use at RAF Locking.

Funded for 5 months from 1 March 1977 at a cost of £6480.

FS 3/02 *Diffusion of CAL to Armed Services Users*

Study base: NDPCAL

This study investigated which military teaching establishments with access to appropriate computing facilities could profitably use packages already developed, or in preparation, in current National Programme projects. Consideration was given to the benefits of such transfers, and to the procedures, staffing, organisation and costing involved in effecting them. Also help was given to the preparation of proposals for other Armed Services projects, particularly with detailed planning for FS 3/03.

Funded for 11 months from 3 March 1975 at a cost of £8387.

FS 3/03A *Simulation and Fault Analysis for Radionics Instruction (SAFARI)*

Study base: RAF Locking, Weston-Super-Mare, Avon

This study is exploring the use of CAL in fault-finding training for RAF maintenance technicians initially working on an airfield radar (AR1). All three Services are interested in the study since the approach could, if successful, have significant implications for other Defence training establishments. The computer provides tutorial and testing sequences as well as simulating fault conditions of the equipment. RAF psychologists are involved in the development of the instructional strategy and the study evaluation. Further trials will apply the system to maintenance training for other equipments and test the ease with which it can be transferred to another computer.

Funded for 1 year from 1 May 1976 at a cost of £16,770.
Extended for 8 months from 1 May 1977 at a cost of £7255.

FS 3/22/01 *Computer Managed Staff Training*

Study base: RAF Staff College, Bracknell, Berks.

This study explored the value of using a computer to manage aspects of the Basic Staff Course which is a short course for squadron leaders. As well as exploring the needs of the Staff College the study contributed to the specification of the general purpose suite of programs for computer managed learning, known as CAMOL, which was being developed centrally (TP 22/02B). It was found that the CAMOL facilities were more extensive than the Staff College required and so the College developed their own system, using MOD funds. The specific need was for automated diagnostic assessment of students on the first day of the course. The system is now in regular use.

Funded for 10 months from 1 January 1974 at a cost of £1177.

FS 3/22/02 *Quality Control in Military Training*

Study base: Trade Training School, 8th Signal Regiment, Catterick, Yorks.

The Trade Training School (TTS) of 8th Signal Regiment is one of the Army's largest technical training establishments with a through-put of about 4000 trainees per annum. A key activity within TTS is assessment of student performance, with the objective of ensuring the highest possible standards of training effectiveness and efficiency. The study will explore the extent to which computer assisted management of learning can meet the current and evolving needs of the school by:

(a) automating the marking and analysis of multiple-choice tests and providing feedback to staff and students
(b) maintaining student records and providing detailed reports for instructional staff and training management
(c) facilitating the use of trade training results in the validation of Army selection procedures.

Following a study of the needs of the School and an evaluation of a number of CML systems in the UK and USA, the ICL Computer Assisted Management of Learning (CAMOL) system is being adapted and implemented on a dedicated ICL 2903 computer. This study is linked with three other CAMOL projects, DP 1/08 at the New University of Ulster, FS 1/22/03A at Brighton Polytechnic and FS 1/22/04 at Bradford College.

Funded for 2 years from 1 January 1976 at a cost of £21,980.

DP 4/01 (FS 4/02) *Management Decision-Making*

Director: P J Boxer, BSc, MSc (London), London Graduate School of Business Studies, Sussex Place, Regents Park, London W1N 4SA. Tel: 01-724 1517

A manager's ability is as much based on his accumulated experience as on what he is taught in formal courses. Thus educational designers have the problem of creating teaching methods which are efficient at conveying factual knowledge but are also capable of involving and developing the manager's experience-based knowledge. The Management Decision-Making Project which addresses this problem grew out of an MSc research project. The teaching methods developed aim to enhance the manager's awareness of the concepts he uses in a decision-making situation and to help him develop those concepts to evolve new ones. Computer-based simulations of various industries and case studies are used to provide contexts for training experiences. Three computer feedback methods based on repertory grid principles have been created to give managers insight into their own decision-making frameworks and enable them to test their understanding of other managers' frameworks.

Project materials have been used in a variety of management courses for institutions and organisations including the National Coal Board, Unilever, Leicester and Central London Polytechnics, and Thames Valley Regional Management Centre. Effort is now concentrated on further dissemination.

Funded for 1 year from 1 February 1975 at a cost of £20,599.
Extended for 1 year 11 months from 1 February at a cost of £71,910.

FS 4/03 *Computer Assisted Post Office Technician Training*

Director: H Blakey, THQ/TP7.1, 16th Floor, St Alphage House, Fore Street, London EC2Y 5XA. Tel: 01-432 3960

This study sought to determine whether the skills which are required by maintenance engineers in the Post Office Telecommunications business can be taught more quickly and effectively using Computer Assisted Training (CAT) techniques to give job-oriented training within a computer managed structure. The Telecommunications Training Division (Engineering Training) with the assistance of other Post Office departments, prepared, ran and evaluated a trial computer assisted course at the Post Office South West Regional Training Centre, Bristol. Four CAT Courses were run and compared with the normal course. Overall student opinion of CAT was favourable and there was some saving of training time. Instructors appreciated the assistance the computer gave to course management but felt they could teach better than the machine. Wider applications and further trials of computer assisted and computer managed methods are planned.

Funded for 1 year 1 month from 1 August 1975 at a cost of £13,868.

TP 22/01 *Cambridge University Transferability Project*

Director: Dr R D Harding, MA, PhD, Dept of Applied Mathematics and Theoretical Physics, Cambridge University, Silver Street, Cambridge CB3 9EW. Tel: 0223 51645

This transferability project assisted in the further dissemination of the experience of the CATAM (*C*omputer *A*ided *T*eaching of *A*pplied *M*athematics) project to other institutions, notably the University of Surrey (see Development Project 1/03A). Both ideas and teaching packages have been successfully transferred, and further experience has been gained concerning the whole question of transferability. The major development at Cambridge was funded from 1969-1974 by the Nuffield Foundation; since 1974 the University itself has funded all the equipment and staff costs through its normal channels.

Funded for 1 year from 1 August 1973 at a cost of £4603.

TP 22/02B *Computer Assisted Management Of Learning* (*CAMOL*)

Director: Mr N J Rushby, BSc, DIC, MBCS

Project base: NDPCAL

A content-free software package CAMOL (specified in Transferability

Project 22/02) has been implemented by a team from ICL to manage a range of learning situations in any subject area. The management functions include:

— assessing students' performance
— keeping records of students' performance and progress through their courses
— advising students on their choice of route through their courses
— reporting to students, tutors and education management on performance and progress.

The system is being tried out at eight educational and training institutions in the UK. The projects — at NUU (DP 1/08), Brighton Polytechnic (FS 1/22/03A), Bradford College (FS 1/22/04) and Catterick (FS 3/22/02) — are described separately.

Funded for 6 months from 12 November 1973 at a cost of £7794.
Extended for 2 years from 1 January 1975 at a cost of £17,955.
Extended for 1 year from 1 January 1977 at a cost of £11,873.

TP 22/03 *BASIC to FORTRAN Machine Translation*

Project base: Culham Laboratory, UKAEA Research Group, Abingdon, Berks. Tel: 0865 41721

This project provides an automatic translation service for programs in a standard set of BASIC into a standard set of FORTRAN, using the Culham ICL 4-70. A pilot translation service is being administered by NDPCAL. To date little use has actually been made of it since it does not seem to be very cost-effective.

Funded for 6 months from 1 April 1974 at a cost of £4409.

TP 22/04A *Physical Sciences Program Exchange* (*PSPE*)

Director: Dr G Beech, PhD, CChem, MRIC, Dept of Computing and Mathematical Sciences, The Polytechnic, Wulfruna Street, Wolverhampton WV1 1LY. Tel: 0902 27371

PSPE has currently 65 members (70:30% UK:abroad). The PSPE library contains over 120 programs, mostly for use in chemistry teaching. 10-15 programs are distributed each month. Annual fees for membership are charged (£25 in UK and Europe; £40 elsewhere), and PSPE aims to be self-financing by the end of 1977. An evaluation of PSPE has shown that the transfer of programs is very cost-effective. The time taken to implement programs locally is far smaller than the time required to develop them from scratch. Currently FORTRAN and ALGOL are the languages used, in batch mode, but BASIC programs are being added in increasing numbers for interactive use. PSPE programs have been implemented on the following machine ranges — ICL 1900; PDP 8,10,11; Interdata; Burroughs 3500 and 6700; IBM 370; Data General Nova; CDC 6600; Xerox 530.

Funded for 2 years from 7 April 1975 at a cost of £8482.
Extended for 35 weeks from 7 April 1977 at a cost of £2960.

TP 22/05 *Havering/Lothian Transferability Project*

Directors: W R Broderick, Head of Educational Computer Centre, London Borough of Havering, Teachers' Centre Annexe, Tring Gardens, Harold Hill, Romford RM3 9QX. Tel: Ingrebourne 49115

P Barker, Centre for Computer Education, Moray House College of Education, Holyrood Road, Edinburgh EH8 8AQ. Tel: 031 556 8455

The Havering Computer Managed Learning System, researched and developed between 1969 and 1976 with the aid of grants from the Social Science Research Council, is a curriculum-independent computer managed learning system. It currently involves courses for teaching respiration and photosynthesis to the third year of secondary schools, as well as tests and a course in teaching the computer language BASIC. The programs were originally written in Hewlett Packard ALGOL but in the course of the transferability project have been rewritten in a highly transportable version of FORTRAN IV. In particular, magnetic peripheral handling, character handling and machine constants have all been removed and put into machine-dependent subroutines. The aim of this transferability project is to transfer the Havering CML system with the biology course materials north of the border for use in Lothian Education Region schools.

Funded for 2 years 6 months from 1 July 1975 at a cost of £15,785.

TP 22/06A *Geographical Association Package Exchange* (*GAPE*)

Director: D R F Walker, MA, MSc(Econ), Loughborough University, Ashby Road, Loughborough, Leics LE11 3TX. Tel: 0509 215751 x 22

Following a design study about program exchanges undertaken for NDPCAL by the National Computing Centre, an operational package exchange scheme under the auspices of the Geographical Association has been established. Existing computer aided geography teaching units from various sources are being demonstrated to teachers, and promoted to encourage greater usage. The problems and costs of transfer are being closely studied. The extent to which computer material is incorporated into teaching schemes is also being investigated. With substantial demand for a package exchange service already demonstrated GAPE will extend the range of packages available and the provision of information and advice.

Funded for 1 year from 1 January 1976 at a cost of £10,006.
Extended for 1 year from 1 January 1977 at a cost of £9878.

Other project summaries

In addition to the 35 main projects summarised above, the National Programme funded four design studies. The summaries of these four design studies, and of one development project (DP 1/05) which was cancelled early in its life, conclude this Appendix.

DS 2/01 *Computer Managed Remedial Reading*

Study consultant: P W Young, Cambridge Institute of Education, Broomfield Place, Main Road, Broomfield, Chelmsford, Essex. Tel: 0245 440506

Study manager: W R Broderick, BSc, FBCS, London Borough of Havering, Educational Computer Centre, Teachers Centre Annexe, Tring Gardens, Harold Hill, Romford RM3 9QX. Tel: Ingrebourne 49115

The design study was a joint exercise between the London Borough of Havering and the Cambridge Institute of Education. The study investigated the educational implications of using the computer managed learning system, developed in the London Borough of Havering Computer Centre, for teaching remedial reading. Curriculum models and content were studied. An educational model for computer managed remedial reading was specified and was then implemented in South Glamorgan (see Design Study 2/02 and Development Project 2/03A).

Funded for 3 months from 1 January 1974 at a cost of £2156.

DS 2/02 *Systems Specification — Computer Managed Remedial Reading*

Consultant Systems Analysts: Langton Information Systems Limited, 74 Newman Street, London W1P 3LA. Tel: 01-580 1036

Following the educational specification for remedial reading made by Mr Peter Young of the Cambridge Institute of Education (see Design Study 2/01) this design study produced a detailed systems specification for the teaching of remedial reading using the computer to aid classroom management. This system specification was programmed as part of Development Project 2/03A.

Funded for 3 months from 1 June 1974 at a cost of £2595.

DS 2/03 *Computer Assisted Learning in Secondary Education*

Consultant: B D C Labbett, NDPCAL

This study examined the feasibility of a development project in geography, economics, history and statistics with fourth- and fifth-year classes in secondary schools, using the computer as a data storage, manipulation and retrieval device.

The final report of the study recommended two feasibility studies — one in quantitative geography at sixth-form level, and one in local studies at lower levels of the secondary school. As a result, three projects were funded: DP 2/05, the Local History Classroom Project; FS 2/03 Computer Assisted Learning in Upper School Geography; FS 2/04 Computer Assisted Learning in Secondary School History.

Funded for 5 months from 1 July 1974 at a cost of £1992.

DS 22/01 *Exchange Systems for Educational Computer Software*

Director: J Turnbull, Head of Educational Applications, National Computing Centre, Oxford Road, Manchester M1 7ED. Tel: 061 228 6333

John Turnbull of the National Computing Centre carried out a one-year investigation on behalf of the National Programme on the nature and extent of usage of educational computing software in the United Kingdom in local-authority-funded establishments, with a view to making recommendations concerning the desirability and means of facilitating the exchange of software. This design study fed into the plans for an aftercare structure for CAL following the end of NDPCAL.

Funded for 1 year from 1 April 1975 at a cost of £15,684.

DP 1/05 *Computer Based Learning Packages*

This project was cancelled within months of starting due to the resignation of the project director. Its aim was to have been the development of computer-based learning packages for use in general science in secondary and further education. Expenditure on the project totalled £4025.

Appendix C: A selected bibliography

General publications on the National Programme

FIELDEN, J and PEARSON, P K (1978) *The Cost of Learning with Computers: Final Report of the Financial Evaluation,* London: CET

HOOPER, R (1974) 'Computers and sacred cows' in Baggaley, J, Jamieson, G H, and Marchant, H (eds), *Aspects of Educational Technology VIII*, London: Pitman

HOOPER, R (1974) 'The National Development Programme in Computer Assisted Learning — origins and starting point', *Programmed Learning and Educational Technology* **11**, 2, and Technical Report No 2, London: National Development Programme in Computer Assisted Learning

HOOPER, R (1975) *Two Years On, The National Development Programme in Computer Assisted Learning: Report of the Director,* London: Council for Educational Technology

HOOPER, R (1977) *The National Development Programme in Computer Assisted Learning, Final Report of the Director,* London: Council for Educational Technology

KEMMIS, S (1975) 'The UNCAL evaluation of computer assisted learning (a case study)' in Stake, R E (ed), *The Responsibility to Evaluate Educational Programs,* Paris: Centre for Educational Research and Innovation, Organisation of Economic Cooperation and Development

KEMMIS, S (1976) *The Educational Potential of Computer Assisted Learning: Qualitative Evidence about Student Learning*, University of East Anglia: Centre for Applied Research in Education

MACDONALD, B *et al* (1978) *Understanding Computer Assisted Learning*, available from the Centre for Applied Research in Education, University of East Anglia, University Village, Norwich NR4 7TJ

MACDONALD, B, JENKINS, D, KEMMIS, S and TAWNEY, D (1975) *The Programme at Two*, University of East Anglia: Centre for Applied Research in Education

MILES, R J (1974) 'National development of computer assisted learning: progress and prospects' in Goos, G and Hartmanis, J (eds), *Lecture Notes in Computer Science 17 — Rechner Gestützter Unterricht (1974)*, pp 397-405, Berlin: Springer Verlag

MILES, R J (1977) *Computers in Industrial Training and Management Development in the 1980s. A Future Study Report,* Technical Report No 19, London: National Development Programme in Computer Assisted Learning

MILES, R J (1977) *Computers in Military Training in the 1980s. A Future Study Report,* Technical Report No 18, London: National Development Programme in Computer Assisted Learning

NDPCAL (1975) *Control and Reporting Systems for Development Projects*, London: National Development Programme in Computer Assisted Learning

NDPCAL (1977) *British Journal of Educational Technology* **8**, 3, special issue on the National Development Programme in Computer Assisted Learning

NDPCAL (1977) *CAL in Higher Education — the Next Ten Years. A Future Study Report,* Technical Report No 14, London: National Development Programme in Computer Assisted Learning

NDPCAL (1977) *Educational Computing in the Local Authority — the Next Ten Years. A Future Study Report*, Technical Report No 15, London: National Development Programme in Computer Assisted Learning

NDPCAL (1977) *Project Summaries and Program Index.* London: National Development Programme in Computer Assisted Learning

Publications about the projects

ABBATT, F R and HARTLEY, J R (1977) 'Teaching applied statistics by computer' in Clarke, J and Leedham, J (eds), *Aspects of Educational Technology X — Individualised Learning,* London: Kogan Page

AYSCOUGH, P B (1976) 'CAL — boon or burden?' *Chemistry in Britain* **12**, 11, pp 348-353

AYSCOUGH, P B (1976) 'Computer assisted learning in chemistry: an exercise in evaluation', *Computers and Education* **1**, 1, pp 47-53

BRODERICK, W R and LOVATT, K F (1975) 'Computer managed learning in the London Borough of Havering', *British Journal of Educational Technology* **6**, 2, pp 71-81

CREASE, A (1977) 'Developing computer assisted learning for undergraduate science teaching' *Physics Education*, January, pp 48-51

DALY, D W, DUNN, W and HUNTER, J (1977) 'The computer assisted learning (CAL) project in mathematics at the University of Glasgow' *International Journal of Mathematical Education in Science and Technology* **8**, 2, pp 145-156

DODD, B (1976) 'Computer assisted learning in nuclear engineering', *Journal of the Institute of Nuclear Engineers* **17**, 5, pp 117-119

HARDING, R D (1975) 'A case study of the use of computer graphics as an aid in applied mathematics teaching' in Lecarme, O and Lewis, R (eds), *Computers in Education,* pp 621-626, Amsterdam: North Holland/American Elsevier

HARDING, R D (1976) 'Evaluative development of a computer assisted learning project', *International Journal of Mathematical Education in Science and Technology* **7**, 4, pp 475-483

HARTLEY, J R (1976) 'Computer assisted learning in the sciences: some progress and some prospects' in Layton, D (ed), *Studies in Science Education* **3**, pp 69-96

HINTON, T, JACKSON, D F, KNIGHT, K R, and CARPENTER, S (1974) 'The role of computer assisted learning in physics teaching', *Proceedings of the 1974 International Conference on Frontiers in Education,* London: Institution of Electrical Engineers

HINTON, T (1977) 'CAL in physics — other approaches', *Physics Education*, March, pp 83-87

HUNT, J W (ed) (1978) *Computers in the Teaching of Local History,* London: Historical Association

LAUNDER, B E, REECE, G J, GOSMAN, A D and LOCKWOOD, C C (1977) 'Computer assisted teaching of fluid mechanics and heat transfer' *Computers and Education* **1**, 3, pp 131-140

LAURILLARD, D (1976) 'The design and development of CAL materials in undergraduate science' in Willoughby, C (ed), *Proceedings of 1976 Conference on Computers in the Undergraduate Curricula CCUC/7,* Library of Congress No 74-10711

LEACH, D F (1974) 'A computer-based laboratory for service mathematics teaching', *Proceedings of the 1974 International Conference on Frontiers in Education*, London: Institution of Electrical Engineers

LEESON, C M (1976) 'Managed mathematics', *Computer Education*, 22, p 19

MCKENZIE, J *et al* (1978) *Interactive Computer Graphics in Science Teaching*, Chichester: Ellis Horwood Limited

MCMAHON, H (1975) 'The computer assisted management of learning in teacher education' in Lecarme, O and Lewis, R (eds), *Computers in Education*, pp 827-832, Amsterdam: North Holland/American Elsevier

MCMAHON, H, BARTON, J and ANDERSON, J (1977) 'Student response to differentiated learning tasks in CML' *Programmed Learning and Educational Technology* **14**, 2, pp 168-175

MURRAY, T S, CUPPLES, R W, BARBER, J H, HANNAY, D R, and SCOTT, D B (1976) 'Computer assisted learning in undergraduate medical teaching', *Lancet i,* pp 474-6

MURRAY, T S, DUNN, W R, CUPPLES, R W, BARBER, J H, and SCOTT, D B (1977) 'The potential of computer assisted learning in undergraduate medical education', *Journal of the Royal College of Physicians* **11**, 4, p 401

PARKER, G R and KNIGHT, K R (1976) 'Can computer assisted learning reduce the cost of equipment training', *Royal Air Force Education Bulletin* **13**

RICHARDS, A J and MCCARTHY, J (1974) 'The Basic Staff Course: training design using the systems approach', *Royal Air Force Education Bulletin* **11**, pp 3-14

RUSHBY, N, MCMAHON, H, SOUTHWELL, A, and PHILPOTT, A (1977) 'Computer assisted management of learning (CAMOL)' in Clarke, J and Leedham, J (eds), *Aspects of Educational Technology X — Individualised Learning,* London: Kogan Page

SMITH, P R (1976) 'Computers in engineering education in the UK', *Computers and Education* **3**, 1, pp 13-21

SPARKES, C A (1975) 'The interactive use of a PDP 11/40 as an instructional aid', *DECUS Europe. Proc DECUS* **2**, 1, pp 311-314

SPARKES, C A (1976) 'CAL — the computer tutor', *Royal Military College Shrivenham Journal*

TAGG, W (1974) 'The Hertfordshire Computer Managed Mathematics Project', *Proceedings of the 1974 International Conference on Frontiers in Education*, London: Institution of Electrical Engineers

TAWNEY, D (ed) (1978) *Learning Through Computers*, London: Macmillan

WALKER, D R F (1976) 'Geographical Association transfer service for computer aided teaching units', *Teaching Geography* **1**, 3, p 140

General publications on computer assisted learning

BEECH, G (ed) (1978) *Computer Assisted Methods in Science Education,* Oxford: Pergamon

COOK, V (1974) *The Human Factors Aspect of the Student/Terminal Interface in Computer Assisted Learning Systems*, Technical Report No

7, London: National Development Programme in Computer Assisted Learning
CORNISH, W (1976) *Legal Aspects of Computer Programs for Education,* Technical Report No 12, London: National Development Programme in Computer Assisted Learning
HOOPER, R (1974) 'Making claims for computers', *International Journal of Mathematical Education in Science and Technology* **5**, 3, pp 359-368
HOOPER, R and TOYE, I (eds) (1975) *Computer Assisted Learning in the UK — Some Case Studies,* London: Council for Educational Technology
HOOPER, R (1976) 'To CAI or not to CAI', *International Journal of Mathematical Education in Science and Technology* **7**, 3, pp 461-473
KNIGHT, K (ed) (1977) *TechnologiCAL. A Future Study Report,* Technical Report No 17, London: National Development Programme in Computer Assisted Learning
MILES, R (1977) 'Computer assisted learning in the Armed Services', *Service Education* 3
OSMON, P (1973) *Terminals for Computer Assisted Learning — Problems and Possibilities,* Technical Report No 5, London: National Development Programme in Computer Assisted Learning
SCOTT, D B (1974) *An Introduction to Computer Graphics,* Technical Report No 6, London: National Development Programme in Computer Assisted Learning
TAWNEY, D (1976) *Simulation and Modelling in CAL,* Technical Report No 11, London: National Development Programme in Computer Assisted Learning

General publications on computer managed learning

BYRNE, C (1975) *Computerised Question Banking Systems,* Technical Report No 10, London: National Development Programme in Computer Assisted Learning
EWART, W (1977) *Computers in Educational Administration,* Technical Report No 20, London: National Development Programme in Computer Assisted Learning
HAWKRIDGE, D (1973) *Problems of Implementing Computer Managed Learning,* Technical Report No 1, London: National Development Programme in Computer Assisted Learning
MILES, R (1976) 'Computer timetabling: a bibliography', *British Journal of Educational Technology* **6**, 3, pp 16-20

RUSHBY, N (ed) (1977) *Computer Managed Learning in the 1980s. A Future Study Report*, Technical Report No 16, London: National Development Programme in Computer Assisted Learning